Armenia

Armenia

Landscape and Architecture

Photos by
Károly Gink

Text by
Károly Gombos

Corvina Press

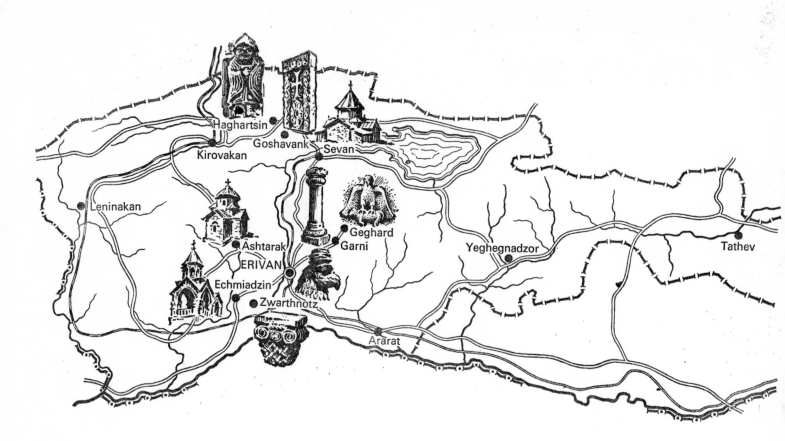

Haghartsin

Goshavank

Kirovakan

Sevan

Leninakan

Geghard

Ashtarak

Garni

ERIVAN

Yeghegnadzor

Tathev

Echmiadzin

Zwarthnotz

Ararat

Contents

Original title:
ÖRMÉNYORSZÁG
Tájak, várak, kolostorok
Corvina Kiadó, 1972

Translated by Rudolf Fischer
Translation revised by Bertha Gaster

Map by Gyula Gáll
Cover, jacket and typography
by István Faragó

Photographs © Károly Gink, 1974
Text © Károly Gombos, 1974

ISBN 963 13 4605 6

Printed in Hungary, 1974
University Printing House, Budapest

A Short Historical Introduction

Moses of Chorene, the fifth century A.D. historian, known as the father of Armenian historiography, has made us familiar with the legend of the origin of the Armenian people. His *History of Armenia* tells of Hayk, Noah's great-grandson, the ancestor of the Armenians, his son Armen and his large family, who fled from Babylon and settled at the foot of Mount Ararat. That was where he established a new home for his people. This story of the Armenian settlement is of course no more than a legend, and the name Armenia can hardly be derived from Armen, but the popular tradition bears witness to the several thousand-year-old history of Armenia.

The highlands of Armenia must be counted among those areas where human civilization first took shape. Archaeological research has provided evidence of agriculture and stock keeping in this region in the stone age, and also that the peoples living there early established contact with Mesopotamia and other slave-owning societies.

Remains from the bronze age indicate a reasonably high level of culture in the highlands of Armenia. The rich mineral deposits of the Caucasus facilitated the manufacture of bronze tools and weapons. The mining of copper and lead on a relatively extensive scale furthered the growth of social life, trade by barter and the development of tribal and clan confederations. Important finds at Dvin, in the Dilizhan area, on the shores of Lake Sevan (in Lchashen) and recently on the hill of Metsamor near Erivan indicate that the ancient peoples of Armenia possessed advanced techniques in the working of metal. A surprisingly large smelting oven was in operation on Metsamor around 2000 B.C. The remaining ruins, such equipment as has survived, slag containing lead and copper, are all so many demonstrations of an advanced standard of metal working techniques. In the first millennium B.C., when the bronze-age culture reached its highest stage of development, they began to work in iron. Tribal confederations were established on the highlands, paving the way to the later organization of states. Archaeological work on the shores of Lake Sevan has revealed the impressively high level of magnificence of this culture.

The ruins of an ancient town excavated near the village of Lchashen have provided an extraordinary amount of new information on the bronze-age culture of the peoples of the Armenian highlands. Finds in princely tombs were particularly interesting. When the waters of Lake Sevan ebbed, remains dating from the twentieth to twelfth century B.C. came to the surface. They included pottery of considerable artistic value depicting various kinds of animals, clay and bronze figures, gold objects, jewellery, various utilitarian bronze objects, arms and wooden carts. One of the tombs appears to have been that of a person of consequence. The remains of thirteen slaughtered slaves and precious jewellery lay around him.

The ancestors of the Armenians, the tribes calling themselves the Hay, lived in the country of Haiasha (Hayasa). Haiasha lay on the banks of the Euphrates, a sovereign state independent of Urartu. Hittite inscriptions of the second millennium B.C. make mention of the country of Haiasha. Hittite, Urartu, Armenian and other tribes all played a part in the development of the Armenian people. The name Armenioi (Armenia) is very probably derived from the tribe of the Arme which lived at the foot of the Taurus. It first occurs in the cuneiform trilingual inscription of King Darius I of Persia of 521 B.C. (Ancient Persian, Mede and Babylonian) on a rock-face at Behistun not far from Kermanshah in Iran.

Assyria lay to the south of the Armenian highlands. From around the middle of the second millennium B.C. the Assyrians regularly raided the highlands for slaves and cattle. Fear of these Assyrian campaigns hastened the process of federation and unification amongst the Armenian tribes. Urartu and Nairi, which occur in Assyrian sources, were in all probability tribal confederations. The whole country acquired the name of Nairi (or the Land of Rivers); according to Assyrian texts there were many cities there, and sixty kingdoms.

The Urartu empire came into being in the ninth century B.C. After ages of unceasing warfare, and attacks by the Medes, it fell apart in 585 B.C. The Armenian tribes living in its area were the inheritors of the culture of Urartu. Arme-Supria, the area of the country inhabited by the Armenian tribes, formed part of Urartu in the eighth century B.C. The Armenian kingdom that took shape later in the sixth century B.C. united the tribes of Haiasha, Nairi and Urartu, and generally speaking this completed the complex process of the formation of the Armenian people, taking place between the twelfth and sixth centuries B.C. It was fostered by the relations which existed between the tribes, by assimilation and by the growth of trade. At this period the Armenians were mainly engaged in agriculture, animal breeding and horticulture. Wheat, barley, sesame seeds and grapes were among their chief crops.

Xenophon and other Greek historians, including Herodotus (fifth and fourth centuries B.C.), make mention of Armenia and report that the Armenians made use of iron implements and that their horticulture and viniculture were highly developed.

Erebuni, 8th c. B.C.
Detail with lion from the frescoes of the fortress

Ashtarak, 7th c.
Carmravor Church and the gate of the fence

Magnificent hill pasture had furthered the development of cattle-breeding. The hill tribes bred superb horses. Xenophon, who had travelled in Armenia, described the country as rich and beautiful. His *Anabasis* describes the Armenian dwellings and various distinctive features of their daily life.

The first Armenian state took shape in the sixth century B.C. under the Ervanduni dynasty. Later Armenia came under the suzerainty of the Persians, and Armenian society evolved under the aegis of the Achaemenid empire.

It was around this time that the basic elements of Armenian epic poetry began to crystallize. Hayk, the mythical ancestor of the Armenians, is displayed fighting the Persian Bel, the Assyrian queen Semiramis is engaged in a life-and-death struggle with the beautiful goddess Ara, and the Armenian kings fight the Persians. These epic tales are a monument to the campaigns waged by the Armenian people against foreign oppressors. Armenians worshipped Hayk, whom they regarded as their first ancestor, and they also sacrificed to Ara, representing the rebirth of nature in the large pantheon of gods and goddesses. These included Astlik, the goddess of fertility, Tork Angel, the god of war, Narini, the goddess of water, as well as good and evil spirits.

The ancient religion of Armenia reflects a powerful Persian influence. The principal god, Aramazd, the Persian Ahuramazda, created heaven and earth, and gave prosperity and courage to mankind. Anahit, his daughter, represented the cult of fertility. The cult of Vaagna was linked with war and heroism. Moses of Chorene relates the legend of a mythical hero who fought the giant monsters which were robbing the earth of the life-giving waters of the sky. At a later period, when Hellenistic culture was spreading, these gods were transformed: Aramazd was changed to Zeus, Astlik to Aphrodite, but the worship of these later gods remained an alien cult in the eyes of the people.

Following the fall of the Achaemenid Persian state the various regions of Armenia were unified in the course of the second and first centuries B.C., though the conquests of Alexander the Great touched on Armenia. This unification within the framework of a Greater Armenia is linked with the Artacesid dynasty. The most famous members of this dynasty were the founder Artaces I (189–161 B.C.) and his grandson Tigranes the Great (Tigranes II; 95–55 B.C.).

Tigranes II embarked on a policy of conquest. He increased the territory of Armenia considerably, and created a unified kingdom extending from the Caspian Sea to the Black Sea and Palestine. He built a new capital, Tigranokert (the present Farkin) in

Mesopotamia, to the north of the Tigris. Tigranes II accepted Hellenistic culture with enthusiasm and did a great deal to further its spread. Armenian cities were built on the Hellenistic model. Greek craftsmen and merchants were encouraged to settle in them and the royal court was a centre of Hellenism.

The state of Tigranes II suffered great losses in the course of sanguinary wars with Rome, but Tigranes the Great was successful in retaining a considerable region of the country under his control. The golden age of Armenia lasted to the end of the fourth century A.D., and the country flourished as one of the greatest of the Hellenistic slave-owning states of ancient times.

The trade route linking the East with Europe passed through Armenia. Armenia consequently carried on a lively trade with both East and West, with Persia, India, China on the one hand, and the Black Sea and Mediterranean ports on the other. Economic life in Armenia throve under the Artacesid dynasty, and later under the Arsacids (63–428). During that period Armavir, Artashat, Vagarshapat, Dvin and many other famous cities on the main trade routes were founded and prospered. The towns of Armenia, famed for their merchants and craftsmen, exported copper, iron, timber, precious stones and metals, pottery, cloth, dyes, cereals, wine, wool and fine horses to distant markets. Trade led to an acquaintance with Eastern and Western culture. The Armenian people soon became familiar with Persian, Chinese, Arab, Indian, Greek, Roman and Byzantine art and economic achievements, and turned them to use in their own country.

It was during the period of the Arsacids that a feudal system came into existence within the framework of a slave-owning society. The peasants, who had until then held land in common, were reduced to a dependent status, in common with the slaves settled on the land. The final imposition and establishment of serfdom was accompanied by violence and unrest, but by the fourth century A.D. most of the land had become the property of the king or the *naharar* (magnates). Thus the whole of the Ararat valley, one of the most fertile areas in Armenia, was owned by the king in the fourth century.

In A.D. 301 Armenia adopted Christianity as the state religion, and was the first country in the world to do so. The king, Tiridates III, and St. Gregory the Illuminator spread the new faith to counteract the doctrines of fire worship in the neighbouring Persian Sassanid empire. The church, developing into a powerful organization, reinforced the ideological and economic basis of the mediaeval state. Weakened by the irresolution and instability of the aristocracy, the country was defeated in A.D. 387. The greater, eastern part came under Persian rule and the western section passed into the possession of the Eastern Roman Empire.

The economic life of the country suffered under foreign domination, and Armenian trade fell away. The role of the towns diminished, the powers of the great landed estates and the castles were extended. The Persians increased the power of the *naharar* (magnates) both politically and economically, but all attempts to turn Armenia into a mere province failed, for the Armenian people successfully resisted both the Byzantine and the Persian policy of assimilation.

A great popular revolt led by Prince Vardan Mamikonian broke out in the middle of the fifth century A.D. Thirty years later Vagan Mamikonian, the nephew of that prince, who had perished in battle, led the peasant rebels against the Persian host. Though practically all the peoples living in the Caucasus joined in the battle, this heroic struggle for independence failed in the absence of outside help.

The Armenian script, invented by Mesrop Maschots in A.D. 396, played a considerable role in the struggle for independence and defence of the national culture. The Armenian people were thus enabled to use their own distinctive script in place of the Greek and Aramaic alphabets previously in use. Daniel, the Bishop of Syria, had earlier attempted to devise an Armenian script, but his experiments had failed. It was Mesrop Maschots's alphabet that finally satisfied the linguistic needs of the Armenian people. The 36-letter alphabet devised by the scholarly monk is still in use today with only minor modifications.

Armenian language schools were founded to encourage the spread of literacy. Distinguished translators, who translated a large number of Syrian, Greek, Persian and other works, were trained in these schools. Mesrop Maschots was followed by a whole series of eminent translators, writers, historians, mathematicians, geographers, philosophers and artists. The most important historians were Agathangelus, Faustus of Byzantium, Koryun, Elisaeus, Lazar of Pharp; the most famous of all was Moses of Chorene, the fifth century historian, called the Herodotus of the Middle East, since his *History of Armenia* provided much useful information about neighbouring countries as well as his own homeland.

The works of the Armenian historians, especially those of Moses of Chorene and Elisaeus, are distinguished by a deep love for their native land and a great sense of literary structure and style. The Invincible David is outstanding among the philosophers; in his *Philosophical Determinations* he discusses the theories of knowledge of the Greek philosophers.

Ananias of Shirak the mathematician was another noted scholar of this period. He was an astronomer and geographer, one of the greatest natural scientists of Armenia, explaining the eclipses of the sun and moon on a scientific basis.

Every aspect of science, scholarship and art developed and flourished between the fifth and the seventh century A.D. Architecture provided masterpieces that were the glory of feudal art.

Armenia was conquered by the Arabs in the seventh century, at the same time as the Persian Sassanid empire. The country suffered under this foreign yoke for over two centuries, from A.D. 652 to 855. The economy declined, the population was decimated, the native Armenians were driven from the land or subjected to unbearable taxation. Arab domination hindered the progress of mediaeval Armenia; commerce and the urban crafts declined, which in turn opened the way to the greater dominance of the military, the noble landowners and the monasteries.

The undaunted struggle of the Armenians for freedom and independence transformed itself into a war of liberation. One revolt after another broke out. The struggle was particularly fierce in the ninth century A.D., when Georgian and Azarbeidjan peasants fought against the Arabs side by side with the peasants of Armenia. *David of Sasun,* 145 the famous Armenian popular epic, recounts the holy war against the Arabs. David, the lord of mountainous Sasun, led the campaign against the Arabs.

Since their power had already been undermined by domestic quarrels between the Umayyad and the Abbasid dynasties, the Arab conquerors were forced to accept the fact that the Caucasian states were gaining increased freedom and later, towards the end of the ninth century, had achieved full independence, and in A.D. 886 the Arabs, in offering the kingship of Armenia to Ashot Bagratian, finally confirmed it. Conditions improved under Bagratid rule. Trade, industry and agriculture flourished, power was centralized under the king, and the anarchy inspired by the great nobles, which had torn the country apart, came to an end.

Ani became the new capital of Armenia under the Bagratids. In the course of the next two centuries it developed into one of the greatest and most beautiful towns of mediaeval times and an important commercial and manufacturing centre, adorned with great palaces and churches and reinforced with a strong fortress. Urban life revived, buildings sprang up throughout the country, with a consequent great impetus to the art of architecture. Internal and transit trade revived in the famous old towns of Dvin, Artashat,

Vagarshapat and others. Trading relations were established with the great Russian trading towns, as for instance Kiev and Novgorod. In the eleventh century Armenia was subjected to attacks by the Seljukid Turks, and in the thirteenth by the Mongols. A considerable proportion of the population of Armenia was forced to abandon their homes; this was the first mass emigration, followed unfortunately by many others.

The Armenian Kingdom of Cilicia, founded on the shores of the Mediterranean in the eleventh century, was the only one to escape devastation by the Mongols, and was able to maintain its independence from 1081 to 1375, when it finally fell in the unequal struggle with the Egyptians.

From the eleventh to the fifteenth centuries foreign invaders trod the soil of Armenia and again inhibited its advancement. These heavy trials failed to break the spirit of the Armenian people; again and again they took to arms against the foreign invaders, supported by all the secular traditions of their national culture. Art and literature played a vital part in keeping the resistance of the people alive. Gregory of Narek (tenth century) was the first outstanding poet of mediaeval Armenia. He wrote secular verse, Nershes Snorhali (twelfth century) wrote religious verse, Mechithar Kosh (twelfth century) wrote tales. One of the greatest and most famous poets of the age was Frik, who lived in the thirteenth century. His work is imbued with revolt against social injustice, hypocrisy, the abuses of power and religious intolerance. A host of philosophers and chroniclers were active in Frik's time and the age that followed. Kirakos of Gandzak was the most important of the historians, and a great deal of valuable information on the social and political life of the Mongol invaders is to be found in his work.

In those difficult days the monasteries situated among remote mountains acted as the havens and depositaries of Armenian culture and art. Building continued in the pauses between each of the devastating wars, and the famous Armenian monasteries multiplied. The well-known monasteries of Gladzor, Ahpat, Sanain, Tathev, Ayrivank and many others flourished, providing both religious and secular education. Gregory of Tathev, who maintained that the world was knowable, taught at the famous Tathev Academy, and Ioan Vorotnetsi, the philosopher, was his contemporary. The monasteries were equipped with libraries and scriptoria. The draughtmanship, directness and originality of colouring of the Armenian miniaturists is inimitable. Toros Roslin and Sarkis Pitzak in Cilicia (thirteenth to fourteenth centuries) were great artists of illumination, but the work of the Van school of illuminators is also highly prized.

Travelling minstrels (gusan), story tellers (vipasan) and poets (asug) were very popular in the countryside, slowly depopulated by these devastating wars. The arrival of a travelling minstrel in a village was always an event; their song was accompanied by instruments, dances and primitive plays. The most popular epic was David of Sasun's fight against the Arabs.

The destructive raids of the Central Asian tribes came to an end at the beginning of the sixteenth century, but a new danger menaced Armenia. The Turks occupied Byzantium in 1453 and Constantinople became the capital of the Turkish empire. Armenia was threatened by Persian expansion in the east and Turkish expansion in the west. The war between the Osmanli empire and Persia led to a great deal of suffering for the Armenian people. Following the peace treaties of 1555 and 1639 the greater part of Armenia came under Turkish rule, while Eastern Armenia was dominated by the Persians. The conquerors showed no mercy to the Armenian people. The Armenians were regarded as unbelievers, slaves and captives, and there was no security for their daily life and labours. The economic and cultural life of the country declined to its lowest level. In those centuries Armenia had the appearance of a devastated country, its agriculture was primitive, and there was practically no industry apart from the domestic handicrafts. From the seventeenth century onwards Armenian culture was fostered and developed abroad in places inhabited by Armenian emigrants. The first Armenian printed books were produced in Venice in 1512, the first map in Armenian appeared in Amsterdam in 1694 and the first Armenian newspaper in Madras, in India in 1794. Armenian schools were founded in Paris, Venice, Calcutta, Astrakhan and Moscow. The most important of them was the Lazarev Academy, founded in Moscow in 1815.

During the Russo-Persian war, at the beginning of the nineteenth century, the Russian army and Armenian volunteers together stormed and took the fortress of Erivan on October 1, 1827. A large part of eastern Armenia, the Erivan and Nakhichevan areas, came under the Russian Czars. A section of the Armenian people was consequently saved from destruction and assimilation under the Persians, but western Armenia continued under foreign domination. An Armenian liberation movement came into being but the response of the Turkish authorities was wholesale massacre.

The massacres of 1894 and 1896, and later those in the course of the First World War, carried out deliberately and systematically, resulted in a million and a half victims, and *143* forced tens of thousands of Armenian families into emigration. The emigrants found

144   refuge in the United States, in France, in Middle Eastern states, in Egypt and in Lebanon. A lasting monument to the Armenian tragedy is to be found in Franz Werfel's famous novel, *The Forty Days of Musa Dagh.*

With the socialist October Revolution of 1917 came the opportunity for the national revival of the Armenian people. Armenia, no more than 'barren earth', has risen again in the past half century. Its economic and cultural achievements speak for themselves. The relatively small Socialist Soviet Republic of Armenia is bounded on the east and north by the friendly Georgian and Azarbeidjan Socialist Republics, on the south by Turkey and Iran. It is 29,800 square km in extent, with a population of 2.1 million. Industry, agriculture, commerce, and dozens of universities, scientific institutions and museums flourish.

The atmosphere in Erivan sparkles as in southern Italy. In 1968 the city celebrated its 2,750th anniversary. Armenian artists, painters, sculptors, architects, composers and actors have placed their best talents at the service of their homeland. Thousands of ancient buildings have been restored and preserved, enabling visitors to enjoy the wonders of Armenian art and civilization down the centuries.

Armenian Architecture

It is in the realm of architecture that the cultural heritage of the Armenian past is best preserved. Fine churches, palaces, castles and other buildings display all the more important stages in the history of an architecture that reaches back several thousand years.

It may sound like a platitude, but it is nonetheless true: Armenia is one great open-air museum. The great number and variety of these monuments provide evidence of the artistic talents of the Armenian people and their creative abilities.

Historians of art and architecture agree that the talent of the Armenian people is best expressed in their buildings; though this is not to say that Armenia has not produced works of significance in painting, particularly in the art of illumination, in the decorative stone sculpture adorning buildings, or in the applied arts.

The great variety of rock and stone suitable for building also helped. Grey and black granites, hard to work, limestone, marble, and rose, yellow, brown and grey porous stone (tufa) which are easy to work were as much at the disposal of builders in ancient times as they are today.

Remains have been found in Armenia dating from the second and third millennia B.C. which indicate that the tribes which settled there tilled the soil and raised cattle. There was such a settlement on Shengavit Hill in the vicinity of Erivan. Gold, silver and bronze objects, as well as pottery, have been excavated near Kirovakan. The excavation of the necropolis near Lchashen on the shores of Lake Sevan has considerably increased our knowledge of bronze-age settlements in Armenia. Carriages made of wood, bronze weapons and implements, jewellery and small bronze figures were found there in tombs. The bronze statuette illustrated in this volume, found at Tolors, also belongs to this culture **18** (tenth century B.C.).

The ruins of Tushpa (on Lake Van), the capital of the Urartu Kingdom, bear witness to the advanced political life, trading and building techniques of the ninth to seventh centuries B.C., as do the fortified towns excavated in the Socialist Soviet Republic of Armenia. These include Armavir, Nor-Bayazet, Covinar, and the strongholds of Arin-Berd (Erebuni) and Karmir-Blur that lie within the present limits of the city of Erivan. These latter have been unearthed, in the course of thirty years' work, by Boris Piotrowski, professor of archaeology, director of the Leningrad Hermitage.

Monastery on the peninsula of Lake Sevan, 9th c.

Haghartsin monastery, 13th c.

Erebuni – Erivan

Erivan, the capital of Armenia, was founded by Argisti I, the Urartu monarch, in 780 B.C. The fortified settlement of Erebuni which he built extended over five acres on the hill of Arin-Berd within the limits of the modern city. Erivan retains the memory of this ancient settlement in its name, and a large number of stone tablets with cuneiform *10–11* inscriptions found during excavations authenticate the tradition of its ancient foundation. A powerful fortress, built in the seventh century B.C., stood on Karmir-Blur ('The Red Hill'), another hill also within the boundaries of the capital.

Excavations at Erebuni have uncovered the ruins of a fortress, a magnificent palace, *1–9* churches and other buildings. The building material used was huge blocks of roughly worked natural stone and mud bricks. Roofs were supported by timber posts resting on stone socles. The roofs were made of timber frames covered in rushes and plastered with mud. The geometric shapes of the buildings recall Assyrian architecture, as do the decorative wall-paintings in the ceremonial reception halls. They show a procession of realistically painted deities, lions, bulls, leopards and dogs. Bright reds and blues predominate on a white ground. The decorative coloured patterns are most interesting and attractive. They consist of stylized flower designs, symmetrical circular compositions, with the occasional use of palm leaves and pomegranates.

Excavations on the banks of the Razdan, on the Karmir-Blur heights in Erivan, were begun in 1939. This is the second, perhaps even more famous fortified settlement of Erivan, Teischebaini, named after Teischeba, the god of lightning and war. It was built about 700 B.C. and was an important link in the Urartu chain of fortifications systematically built on prominent peaks in the Armenian mountains. They are all on important crossroads, and give a clear view in all directions. The location of the fortresses was thus determined by strategic consideration.

12–15 Teischebaini was the residence of the Urartu governor. A fairly large garrison was stationed there. The settlement consisted of a fort, the fortified walls that surrounded it, and a small town stretching between the western and the southern strongholds. The fortress had an area of approximately four acres, the town itself covered roughly a hundred. A wall also surrounded the town, strengthened with bastions. The regular arrangement of the dwellings leads to the conclusion that the town was built according to a predetermined plan.

The fortress and the palace of the governor have been excavated, and a great number of smaller and larger rooms dug out. The rooms were not particularly large, some no wider than three or four metres, and the great hall was over thirty metres long and more than ten metres wide. Its roof was supported by three large brick columns.

Large ceramic vessels with a capacity of several hundred litres each were found in the great hall, half-buried in the floor. They may have been containers for oil or wine. In fact this hall may possibly have been the wine cellar of the fortress. Horticulture and viniculture had reached an advanced state of development in Urartu.

Most of the works of art found during the excavations at Teischebaini are on display in a permanent exhibition at the Armenian Historical Museum in Erivan.

Urartu flourished between the ninth and tenth centuries B.C. Some of the finest Urartu work was done by first-class workers in metal. They made very fine weapons, helmets and swords. Considerable quantities of bronze armour, shields, helmets and other objects were also found in Teischebaini, which were remarkable for the delicacy of the metal-work. The friezes of lions or bulls are very striking. Another popular subject was horses harnessed to chariots. Assyrian sources in fact mention that the Urartu were famous for the horses they bred and their staying power. Urartu cattle-breeding was also well-developed, witness the holy bulls depicted on the friezes of buildings, on utilitarian vessels, the handles of cauldrons for instance. Weapons were decorated with the images of gods, the tree of life, winged genii, soldiers and war chariots.

They were skilled in casting figures in bronze. Figurines, designed monumentally in simple massive forms, have been discovered representing the members of the Urartu pantheon: Teischeba, the god of thunder and war, with a peculiar smile on his face, Kaldi, the god of the sky, the principal god, Siuini, the god of the sun, and others.

Assyrian sources inform us that larger bronze statues were to be found in the Temple *17–18* at Musasir, which was built in the eighth century B.C. Large stone figures were rare. *16* Objects, statues and even furniture decorated with figure work were covered in gold foil. Human faces and animal heads were made from white stone, eyes and eyebrows shaped from various coloured stones. Their jewellery, especially the goldsmiths' and silversmiths' work, was outstanding. Magnificent gold and silver jewellery depicting gods was found at both Teischebaini and Erebuni.

This highly developed Urartu culture was influenced by the art of a number of ancient Eastern countries. Assyria took first place, but Egypt also made its influence felt, through Syria and the Hittites. The winged genii suggest a link with Mediterranean countries. The advanced techniques of Urartu iron and metalwork in their turn influenced the

Transcaucasian peoples and the Scythians, since Urartu metalwork had reached the Scythians living on the north shores of the Black Sea in the course of trade.

Urartu techniques of irrigation, agriculture, horticulture, cattle-breeding, architecture and craftsmanship in general were inherited by the people of the Caucasus, who established independent states of their own in the fourth–third centuries B.C. after the destruction of Urartu around 585 B.C. as a result of attacks by the Scythians and the Medes.

Garni

There are no comprehensive works dealing with buildings dating from the period when the Armenians first came into being as a people (sixth to third century B.C.). The detailed study of this period is a task which awaits the future. It is well known from ancient sources, however, that Hellenistic culture flourished in Armenia in the third and second centuries B.C., i.e. when the Armenian state itself took shape. Armavir, Artashat, Ervandasat and Karkatiokert were all centres of Hellenism, as was the famous city of Tigranokert, founded by Tigranes II. The great traditions of Hellenistic culture flourished in Armenia as late as the early centuries of the Christian era, as can be seen from Garni. Garni, the famous ancient fortress, and the village bearing the same name, are 28 km from Erivan. It extends over roughly eight acres and is one of the most important historical sites of Armenia. The beauty of the landscape, and the impregnable strength of the fortress were both famous in ancient times.

The fortress is situated near the valley of the Azat, a mountain stream, on a triangular rocky plateau. To the south and south-east it is surrounded by fearful chasms; at certain points the precipice on which it stands drops 300 metres to the depths. The other sides of the plateau are surrounded by strong defensive walls and four-sided bastions. They resemble in shape the Hellenistic towns and defences built by the Urartians. The fourteen bastions are situated at 25 to 32 metres from one another along the section of the wall most easy to defend. In places where stronger attacks could be expected the bastions were placed closer to one another at every 10 to 13.5 metres. Natural obstacles also helped to defend the entrance to the castle. The rocky terrain only gave access to the enemy in small numbers at a time.

The walls and bastions were built of large bluish-grey granite blocks quarried in the neighbourhood. The carefully hewn blocks were further reinforced by iron couplings. At more important points, such as corners, the holes bored for the couplings were also filled with molten lead. The walls were more than two metres thick and the bastions over three metres in diameter.

The fortifications are in ruins, but they nevertheless provide a clear picture of their state as they once must have been. In some places the walls are still six to eight metres high. It therefore seems no exaggeration to assume that the walls near the entrance were originally more than 20 metres high. The west and north-west walls have largely collapsed. One can see that there the lead-fillings have been removed. They were probably used for military purposes.

Opinions differ as to the date when Garni was built. The general consensus of scholars holds that the fortress was probably already in existence in the third century B.C.; they assume that it was built either early in the period of the Artacesid Kingdom, or else in the Ervanduri era.

The policy followed by the ruling house placed Armenia under the influence of Hellenistic culture in the third and second centuries B.C., and an aristocratic culture flourished in Armenia as in other eastern countries that came under Hellenistic influence. Many representatives of Hellenistic culture were given refuge in Armenia in the reign of Tigranes II (95–55 B.C.). Amongst them were Amphicrates, a writer who fled from Athens, and Metrodorus, the philosopher and historian. Native Armenians also played their part in the triumph of Hellenism at the royal court, such as Artavasdes II, the son of Tigranes, who wrote tragedies and other works in Greek. Garni was one of the centres of this aristocratic Hellenistic culture; another was the city of Artashat, called from its beauty the 'Armenian Carthage' at the time.

The earliest written reference to Garni comes to us from Tacitus, the Roman historian (first century A.D.) speaking of a palace revolution there. Describing the wars that followed he mentions the siege of Garni, and declares that it was taken through treason in 51 A.D.

M. Sarian, the Armenian painter, and a companion found a Greek inscription on a stone in the churchyard of Garni. This inscription has been most valuable in enabling us to understand the history of the building of the castle and its reconstruction on a number of occasions. Part of the inscription has unfortunately perished, and opinions are not unanimous on the interpretation of what has survived. One thing is certain: the fortress was reconstructed in the eleventh year of the reign of King Tiridates I, that is in 77 A.D. This date is supported by a payment of 50 million drachmas made by Emperor Nero to King Tiridates I of Armenia in 65 or 66 A.D. as a contribution towards the rebuilding of the city of Artashat, destroyed by Roman forces in 59 A.D. It is probable that rebuilding also went on at Garni at the same time as Artashat was reconstructed, since Garni had suffered considerable damage in the wars.

Moses of Chorene, the fifth-century historian, also mentions the famous fortress. According to him it was built in the reign of Tiridates III (287–330 A.D.). It is however quite clear that it was built far earlier. Other fifth-century chroniclers describe Garni as a very well-fortified castle (Faustus of Byzantium), or an impregnable stronghold (Elisaeus).

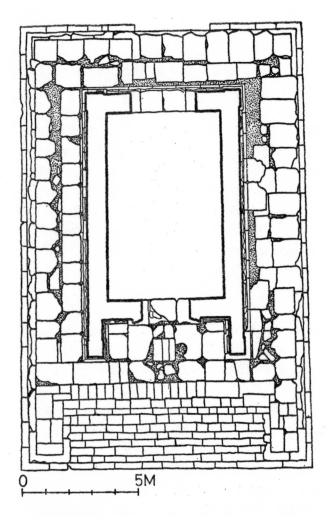

Garni. Ground-plan of the ancient temple

0   5M

Seventh-century sources speak of Persian forces being stationed there (Sebeos). In the course of time the settlement ceased to be a fortress. Historians from the tenth to the thirteenth century refer to Garni as a town containing a variety of traders and merchants. There is evidence of building right up to the beginning of the seventeenth century, as late as 1605, when Shah Abbas of Persia ravaged Armenia and forcibly transferred the population of Garni to Persia. The area was depopulated, and life in the Azat valley only revived two centuries later, when Eastern Armenia was annexed by Russia.

Excavations at Garni were carried out under the direction of Academician N. Marr between 1909 and 1911. Work was taken up again in 1949, under the direction of Professor B. N. Arakelian, and has continued to this day. It has been established that the castle underwent five periods of reconstruction between the third century B.C. and the age of the Zaharid dynasty in the 13th century. The system of fortifications, ancient temples and baths, the palace and early Christian remains have all been excavated.

21 *Ancient temple.* The pagan temple found at the highest point of the rocky plateau dominates the landscape and the castle. This majestic temple stands in perfect harmony with the landscape of strangely shaped hills which surround it. From whichever point we approach it, it is the temple's festive appearance that first catches our eye.

A small picturesque vineyard stands behind the temple, backed by the steep drop of the precipice. The three hundred-metre high wall of rock falls to the valley of the Azat.

The precise date of its construction has not so far been established. The majority of scholars believe that it was built in the second half of the first century A.D. It is possible that it was founded by King Tiridates I, and was devoted to the worship of the sun. This hypothesis appears to be confirmed by old historical sources and by a survey and analysis of the building itself.

Armenia contained a fair number of pagan religious sites. The majority of these buildings were demolished by King Tiridates III following the establishment of Christianity in the country towards the end of the third and the beginning of the fourth century, and replaced by churches in which the new god was worshipped on the same site. According to Moses of Chorene this particular temple was converted into a summer residence for the sister of King Tiridates III. Many have thrown doubt on this statement by the well-known fifth-century historian. It is generally accepted, however, that a royal palace existed there already in the first century A.D., and it may well be that the well-defended fortress and the beautiful climate together led to Garni being used as a summer residence by the kings of Armenia.

Christianity began to spread in Armenia towards the end of the second century A.D. and became the state religion at the beginning of the fourth century. In all probability the pagan statues were removed from the temple and the old building turned into a royal audience chamber, surviving in good repair right to the seventeenth century.

These ancient ruins have aroused the interest of many well-known scholars and travellers from Russia and other countries. A major earthquake destroyed the temple in 1679. Nonetheless, basing himself on what remained, Professor N. G. Buniatian was able to draw up plans in 1931 for its reconstruction, with only a very small margin of error.

Professor Buniatian also directed conservation work in the nineteen thirties. The temple is half in ruins today, but all the necessary elements are there and the work of reconstruction is being carried on under the direction of an architect, Alexander Sainian. *24*

The temple is of the *peripteros* type, that is to say, in the Graeco-Roman style, surrounded by a row of columns. It was probably a temple dedicated to Mithras, the god of the sun. The shorter sides had six columns each, the longer ones eight. Its small size (5.14×7.92 metres) leads one to assume that the space within was only used to hold the statues, and the ceremonies of worship took place outside. The main façade faced north, which is where the only entrance was situated. The temple stood on a high platform, and nine steps, each of them 30 cm high, led up to the entrance, giving the small building a majestic and ceremonial appearance. The columns were decorated with reliefs on both sides, kneeling Atlases supporting something heavy. Sacrificial vessels were probably placed on the columns above them. *22*

The walls of the temple were built of beautifully worked bluish-grey granite. The craftsmen who carved the hard, difficult granite were in all probability Armenians. Centuries-old traditions in the working of local stone were at their fingertips, and they had also inherited the technical expertise of the Urartu. Armenian craftsmen were familiar with the form of Hellenistic temples and other buildings, and with Hellenistic art in general. The decorative motifs used, such as the variety of acanthus, and local folk motifs, including the pomegranate and the vine, suggest local craftsmen, and their wealth of variety indicates an eastern influence. Colour and variety characterised eastern art, as simplicity characterised Graeco-Roman traditions. *25–30*

The construction of the temple as such, its particular formal qualities, the harmonious relationship of the parts to the whole, establish a connection with the temple at Pergamon, and the decorative elements show an affinity with the art of Syria.

The ruins of a four-roomed third century bath are to be found fifty metres from the temple. A mosaic floor composed of local coloured pebbles represents subjects from Greek mythology. *20*

Armenian rug with traditional patterns

St. Luke the Evangelist
Detail of miniature in an illuminated Gospel from Koranatshat, 1224
Matenadaran, Codex No. 4823

Echmiadzin (Vagarshapat)

The beginnings of Armenian architecture, and the development of particular national styles in art coincide with the spread and establishment of Christianity. Some of the ancient temples were probably converted and adapted to church purposes. These questions have not yet been cleared up in a satisfactory fashion. One thing is certain: the early Christian churches were of the basilica type, and the styles of Syria and Asia Minor left their mark on them. Buildings with central domes appeared simultaneously with basilicas in the sixth century, and spread early in the seventh century. The cathedral at Echmiadzin is one of the archetypes of this style.

The town of Echmiadzin, known as Vagarshapat until 1945, is 20 km from Erivan, the capital.

Vagarshapat is an ancient town. It came into being in the second century A.D., at the time of King Vagarshak of Armenia, on the site of Vardkesevan, a well-known settlement which was in existence as early as the second century B.C., and according to some sources even in the third century B.C.

Moses of Chorene mentions the building of the town, reporting that King Vagarshak built walls and ramparts and named the place Vagarshapat or Nor-Kahak (i.e. New Town). Agathangelus, another Armenian historian, also mentions the building of the town. He describes the main roads and gates, and the country surrounding it. No natural features gave protection to the town, unless the marshes to the south-west can be regarded as a form of defence. The Metsamor, a small stream, flows to the south, and there are vineyards on the north-eastern side. After the Roman legions had overcome Armenian resistance in 163 B.C. the conquerors, however, probably selected the town as their seat on account of its fortifications and favourable geographic position. From that moment until 387, Vagarshapat was the capital of Armenia, and later became its religious centre.

Following devastation by the Persians, the seat of the church was transferred to Dvin, the new capital, in the second half of the fifth century A.D.

The seventh century A.D. was a period of vitality and animation in mediaeval Armenian culture, not least in architecture.

A great deal of building was carried on in Vagarshapat and its surroundings during the seventh century. Great churches were built in honour of the martyrs Ripsime and Gaiane, to replace the earlier simple temples. The magnificent church of Zwarthnotz, and the residence of the Catholicos Nerses III were not far from the town.

The town was occupied by the Arabs around the middle of the seventh century A.D., and Vagarshapat declined and lost its earlier importance. When the Arabs were finally expelled it revived under the Bagratid dynasty.

The monastery, the cathedral and the bishop's palace of Echmiadzin were the centre of the religious life of Armenia from the beginning of the fourth to the twelfth century. Following the devastating raids of the Mongols, the seat of the church was transferred to Sis in Maritime Armenia, in the Armenian kingdom of Cilicia. After the fall of Cilicia, Vagarshapat once again became the centre of church life, beginning with the middle of the fourteenth century, and has retained that position to this very day.

The importance and landed wealth of the Monastery of Echmiadzin steadily increased together with the number of monks, and as a result building never ceased, despite the difficult times that followed the loss of independence. The Armenians suffered greatly from the oppression of the foreign conquerors, but even under their rule Echmiadzin remained the spiritual and intellectual centre of Armenia. In 1827 Eastern Armenia was annexed by the Czars of Russia, and life in the town revived. The town was rebuilt under the Soviets. S. Manukian, the Soviet-Armenian architect, produced a plan for the town in 1939, but modern developments have long ago outgrown it. The town, in which only a few hundred people lived not so long ago, now has 20,000 inhabitants, and many thousands of visitors come from Armenia itself and from abroad.

Fifth century Armenian chroniclers date the construction of the first Christian church *31* in Echmiadzin as in the beginning of the fourth century A.D. at the time of King Tiridates III and St. Gregory, the Apostle of Armenia.

The *History of Armenia* by Agathangelus, the fifth century historian, is full of interesting tales about the conversion of the Armenians to Christianity and other events in the third and fourth centuries. The historian recounts a legend of the building of the cathedral. Christ, it is related, appeared in a dream to St. Gregory, holding a burning hammer, and pointing to the spot where the church should be built. This legend explains the name of the cathedral: Echmiadzin means the place where the Lord's only begotten son descended to earth.

The cathedral has been rebuilt a number of times in the more than fifteen hundred years of its existence. Its exterior has been considerably modified, the ensemble of buildings have lost any coherent character, and every major period in the history of architecture has left its mark on it.

The first important reconstruction took place towards the end of the fifth century, in the time of Prince Vagan Mamikonian. Some argue that it was at this time that it was transformed into a building with a central dome. Prior to that period it had probably been a church with a long nave like most other early Christian churches. Four columns divide the interior; they are linked by arcades, and the dome is in the centre. The ground-plan and interior proportions of the church are admirable in their harmony, and there is a consistent relationship between the parts and the building as a whole.

The church as it stands today has a central dome. Whether the original cathedral was in the form of a basilica or a church with a domed crossing surmounted by a drum is a question still to be solved by experts. Toros Toramanian, a historian of architecture, considers that the ground-plan of the church was probably rectangular, with four semi-circular chapels. Five domes covered the church, the largest at the centre, the four smaller ones at each corner. Alexander Sainian directed the excavations which took place in the 1950s, during repairs, and discovered objects around the foundations which rebut arguments for a fourth-century central plan. The church therefore was not probably built originally as a basilica. Whatever the truth of the matter, the facts indicate that the cathedral of Echmiadzin played an important part in the development of churches with central domes in Armenia. Recent researches show quite certainly that this type of ground-plan first came into being and then spread in the area of the Caucasus in the closing years of the sixth century A.D. and even more in the seventh century. What must be emphasized here is the integration of chapels with clover-leaf ground-plans and a central dome, which became first a local peculiarity, and later the Middle Byzantine style, particularly in evidence in the monasteries on Mount Athos. This type of church was perfected in the seventh century, and Armenia possesses a great number of variations on this type. The seventh-century Ripsime and Gaiane churches are magnificent examples of this type in Echmiadzin itself. The Avan church near Erivan is similar, but older, going back to the sixth century. Churches at Targmanchak-vank, Aramus, Mastara, Bagavan and many others also belong in this category.

The rebuilding of the cathedral, begun in the fifth century, in the time of Prince Vagan Mamikonian, was not completed. It was continued in the first half of the seventh century by the Catholicos Komitas (612–621), and by Nerses III 'the Builder' (641–661). Toros Toramanian believes that the cathedral took on its present appearance at this time, and that it has been preserved from that period without major changes. It was around this time that the chapels came to be placed outside the foundation walls, and that the timber roof of the cathedral was replaced. The church has three entrances, the fourth, on the southern side, was walled up. The main western door leads to the altar. The western, southern and northern chapels are five-sided on the exterior. There are altars on two sides of the eastern apse, and the sacristy has been built beside it.

Reconstruction and repair work of the cathedral of Echmiadzin began again in the seventeenth century when monastic life once more began to flourish. Several monastic buildings were erected at the same time, and the whole group of buildings was surrounded by a wall. It was at this time that the cathedral lost some of its oldest and most characteristic features. A thorough reconstruction was made necessary by damage to the walls in various places, the roof and the dome had collapsed, and the flooring also showed gaps. Practically every Catholicos in the seventeenth century contributed to the work of reconstruction, while putting up new buildings at the same time. The Catholicos Philippos, who occupied the episcopal throne in 1633, also built extensively. The construction of the campanile to the west of the church was begun in his time, in 1653. It was completed under the Catholicos Hakop Djugaetsi in 1658.

The campanile is a beautiful piece of work in its own right. Together with the stone *32* carvings which adorn it, it must be regarded as an outstanding product of the Armenian seventeenth-century architecture. The later style in which it was built, however, is not in keeping with the general aspect of the ancient cathedral. This dissonance was also noted by V. M. Arutiunian, the Armenian architectural historian, who is a well-known expert on Echmiadzin. The stone carvings appear to be too flamboyant, too ornate, for the *38–40* appearance of the ancient church. The reds and browns of the stones of the campanile only serve to heighten the contrast with the dark grey—blackening with age—of the cathedral.

In 1869 a building designed to house church treasures and vessels was erected to the east of the cathedral. Today it is in use as a museum for Armenian religious and ap- *33–34* plied art. *36–37*

Echmiadzin is traditionally the spiritual and artistic centre of the Armenian people. The first printing press was established in the monastery, and many outstanding figures in the world of Armenian scholarship and culture worked there, among them Comitas, the great composer, musicologist and ethnographer, who went insane after witnessing the Armenian massacres in Turkey in 1915.

Members of the eminent Ovnatanian family of painters worked on the cathedral for over a century. In 1720 Nagash Ovnatanian was invited to cover the interior and the dome with frescoes. His grandson, Ovnatan Ovnatanian, lived at the royal court in Georgia, and was the contemporary of Saiat-Nova, the famous Armenian poet and singer. He continued the work of his ancestors, painting not only religious subjects but also numerous portraits. He also restored the Catholicos' collection of paintings. Ovnatanian's paintings disappeared in the nineteenth century under a layer of whitewash covering the whole interior of the church. Not so very long ago, specialists working in 1955 and 1956 under the direction of Lydia Durnovo, an art historian, restored the work of the Ovnatanian, showing the characteristic marks of late Persian art, to its original splendour. The effect of these wall paintings, with their use of foliate designs, flowers and wreaths, is very oriental. The strong colours, the spaciousness of the design, recall the eastern style.

35, 43

45–46

The last and most important restoration work on the cathedral was carried out between 1955 and 1965. The other monastic buildings were restored at the same time, and new ones were built. The Catholicos' palace is part of the monastery, and so is the famous Tiridates gate, the guest hostel, the monastic school and the refectory, as well as the small artificial lake, which is very popular with the inhabitants of Echmiadzin.

Ashtarak

The town of Ashtarak, one of the oldest settlements in Armenia, lies along the steep banks of the Kasakh, 22 km from Erivan. Well-irrigated orchards form part of the picturesque landscape which surrounds this small historic town.

The fifth century Ciranavor basilica is the oldest building of the town in good repair, and an important specimen of early Christian architecture. Four columns divide the interior into three aisles. It is a modest building, but its solid walls create the impression of a fortress. The dark tufa walls, the small windows and austere decoration heighten this impression of simplicity. It would appear that the basilica has been restored and altered a number of times on the evidence of the stone cladding of the dome and the variety of colours on the walls, but this multicoloured effect in no way detracts from the ancient character and majesty of the church. The massive walls surrounding it suggest that the church on the banks of the river served on occasion as a refuge for the inhabitants of the region.

The Carmravor Church was built in the seventh century. This small martyrium (6 × 7.5 *53–55* metres) is one of the most beautiful examples of a building with a central dome in Armenia. What is particularly interesting is the survival of the seventh century tiled roof intact, the only one of its kind in Armenia. There are indications from certain sources, however, that the church may have been rebuilt in the tenth century and that the present roof originated at that time. The elongated drum supporting the dome bears out this suggestion. The attractive roof tiles were embedded in lime mortar and strengthened by roof-nails. The entrance is on the western side. Interior arcades are supported by columns, and the drum of the dome rests on the arcades, as does the unusual helmet-shaped roof. The supporting columns do not in fact bear the weight of the structure, their purpose is rather to give a certain lightness to the design and to increase the architectural effect. This kind of structure is fairly common in the Caucasus. From a distance the church gives the appearance of having been carved out of a single rock, thus confirming the picture given by many art historians in their descriptions of Armenian churches in general. The sculptured effect is increased by the isolated position of the church. It is surrounded only by a few hachkars (stone crosses), the most notable of them being the Cakkar (stone with a hole). It owes its name to the opening under its base. According to the inscription on it, it was erected by a priest in 1268.

The church at Carmravor was probably devoted to dynastic purposes, and was in all likelihood a mausoleum. This argument is supported by the cruciform ground-plan, and by the absence of decoration. The window frame and the plaited ornamentation deserve mention as well as the inscription giving the date and details of its foundation. The

56–57 majority of the inscriptions and crosses on the wall date from a much later period.

The design and ground-plan of the Carmravor Church are closely related to the Arsacid mausoleum in the village of Ahc (fourth century) and to the small church, also serving dynastic purposes, built by Prince Kamsarakan of Talin in the closing years of the seventh

47–48 century. All three are cruciform in plan. A small fifth or sixth century early Christian church at Parbi can also be included in this group.

58 The seventeenth century Ashtarak bridge climbs in steps over its three arches to the much higher left bank. It is 17 metres long and five metres wide. The solid balustrade follows the line of the bridge. The left of the biggest arch is decorated with a puffin. The remains of an older bridge are visible in the vicinity.

In the old Armenian villages in the neighbourhood of the town of Ashtarak, famous for their vineyards, a great number of historical monuments are found. Close by Ashtarak

49–52 lies the village of Mogni. Its church, in the style of the ancient Armenian cathedrals, was built by the architects Saak Hizani and Murat from 1661 to 1669.

The western side of the ancient St. George Church is decorated with an open gallery. The portal in the southern side rivals the beauty of the western gate. The decoration and stone carvings of the portal made lavish use of Armenian folk motifs. The high dome and the windows divide the wall surface of the large drum of the dome evenly. The interior of the church is decorated by frescoes.

The greatest beauty of the St. George Church lies in the varied colour of the stone. The architects made brilliant use of the decorative opportunities provided by different coloured tufas.

Zwarthnotz

One of the most interesting of the mediaeval Armenian churches, St. Gregory of Zwarthnotz (the Church of the Guardian Angels), lies along the road to Echmiadzin, 18 km from Erivan.

The very choice of the site reveals a sensitive appreciation of the environment. The Great and Little Ararat, permanently covered by snow, rise behind the church. Orchards of walnuts, apricots, pears and mulberries, vineyards and groves of poplars surround the ruins.

The episcopal palace church of Zwarthnotz was built between 643 and 652 by the Catholicos Nerses III, who is often called The Builder because of his passion for architecture. Nerses III was philhellene in his sympathies and was anxious to strengthen Byzantine influence in Armenia. This is indicated by the inscription in Greek in the church.

The magnificent round church, and the bishop's palace beside it, were already in ruins by the tenth century. Whether this was due to faulty construction, an earthquake or devastation by the Arabs is still an open question.

There is a tradition that the alien conquerors forced three thousand Armenian captives to tear down the capitals of the columns, using hammers and chisels. The marks of violent blows on the capitals can indeed still be seen.

The ruins were buried in a thick layer of earth, and for many years their existence was unsuspected. Archaeological work on the site began in 1900 and continued until 1907. The foundations of the church emerged almost intact, as well as considerable remains of columns and capitals. The capitals are decorated with the traditional Armenian pomegranates, grapevines and bunches of grapes, and reliefs portraying workers wielding spades, hammers and other tools adorn the outer side of the arcades. The capital showing Master Ioann holding a tool was also found. Tradition has it that he built the church. Twenty-eight reliefs decorated the outside walls of the church, but the Catholicos following Nerses III removed those with representations of the master builders, objecting to the honour paid them.

There are still a number of problems connected with these magnificent reliefs of Zwarthnotz. Some scholars maintain that the figures represent gardeners and vintners, arguing that the tools they hold are implements used in viticulture. The subject of these reliefs may well be in dispute, but their artistic value is beyond argument. The clothes and tools tell us a great deal about the seventh century. They indicate considerable skill and artistic power in the management of figures, and also reveal that characters and themes from secular life formed part of the subject-matter of ecclesiastic art.

Fragments of a relief from the Zwarthnotz cathedral, 7th c.

St. Mark the Evangelist
Detail of miniature from an illuminated Gospel, 1304
Nakhichevan school
Work of Master Simeon
Matenadaran, Codex No. 3722

Zwarthnotz.
Cross-section of the cathedral

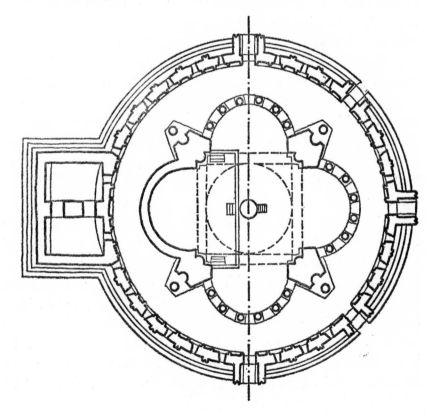

0   5   10M

Ground-plan
of the cathedral

The architectural ornamentation of Zwarthnotz was so rich and varied that a description of the individual carvings in stone would fill volumes. The intention behind them was to uplift the faithful with the sight of magnificent and noble images and objects of beauty. Elaborate designs decorated the capitals of the columns, the arcades, the door jambs *62–69* and the window-frames. Carved palmettes, an eagle with outspread wings, Armenia's heraldic beast, not to mention a large variety of geometrical patterns, were also carved on the exterior, but we can be certain that the interior was equally rich as proved by fragments that have been found, and the interior must have been filled with mosaics and wall-paintings, stone-carving and pottery.

The noble and monumental ruins in Zwarthnotz remind the visitor of the Pantheon in Rome. It is understandable that a number of famous Armenian architects were haunted by a vision of the reconstruction of the cathedral. Toros Toramanian, who took part in the excavations after 1904, prepared a sketch of a possible reconstruction in 1905. According to him the cathedral was a round basilica with a nave and a central dome. Many doubted on Toros Toramanian's plan of reconstruction at the time, until an expedition led by Academician N. Marr excavated a similar, but later, eleventh century church in Ani (1905–1906). The views of Toros Toramanian, a great scholar and architect, were confirmed, although the latest researches indicate modifications, at least in the details, in his reconstruction of the shape of the round church. The diameter of the church was 33.75 metres; that of the Pantheon in Rome is 43.3 metres. The interior was broken by columns and altar-niches. According to Toros Toramanian the building was 45 metres high, according to S. Mnatsakanian only 36 metres. S. Mnatsakanian prepared plans for its reconstruction in 1958. This plan equally assumes that the ground-plan of the cathedral was round, built in three ascending tiers, topped by a dome, but his sketch indicates that the mass of the four altars was clearly separated from the circular interior space of the building. The design retained the traditional cruciform ground-plan. The *61* cross, Mnatsakanian considered, was outlined in the semi-circular space between the lines of the columns. The church was circular on the outside. The composition is simple and original. The various levels mount like an upright telescope up to the dome. The lower sections of the columns have survived to our day. Their size is surprising, and it is a quite reasonable suggestion, put forward by certain architects, that they were over 20 metres high. Small columns filled the space between the large ones, the apses were placed between them. Two galleries ran round the interior. The main altar was to the east. The walls were covered with paintings and mosaics.

70–78 Zwarthnotz cathedral was a magnificent building and represented a great step forward in Armenian mediaeval architecture. It embraced the earlier national achievements in architecture, and took them further. This new and audacious building had a considerable effect on the architecture of both the Armenians and the neighbouring peoples, though few similar buildings exist beyond the Caucasus. Four churches of this kind have so far been found south of the Caucasus, all influenced in their design by Zwarthnotz. The best known is in Ani, the famous capital of mediaeval Armenia. This church, consecrated to St. Gregory, was built in the eleventh century, when Zwarthnotz was already in ruins. The effect of Zwarthnotz was very great not only on contemporary architecture but on later churches as well.

79 The episcopal palace of the Catholicos and the administrative buildings were some 15 metres from the cathedral. The scale of the remains of its halls, baths and other offices confirm the belief that the palace was a worthy companion to this great building.

The objects on display at the museum near the ruins (opened in 1937) are in themselves evidence of the greatness of Zwarthnotz, and its influence on Armenian craftsmanship which reached a high artistic level, particularly in the art of manuscript illumination. The Armenian chronicler, Moses Kalankatuatzi, recorded that the Byzantine Emperor Constantine III attended the consecration of the cathedral in A.D. 652. The Emperor was greatly impressed by the beauty of the church, and desired to take the builders back to Constantinople with him, and there build a round church similar to the one at Zwarthnotz. According to the chronicle the aged master builder died on the way, and the wishes of the Emperor were consequently frustrated.

Even in its ruins Zwarthnotz bears witness to the artistic powers and cultural heritage of the peoples of the Caucasus. The culture which developed there cannot be simply regarded as nothing more than an offshoot of the great culture of Byzantium. The ancient churches of Armenia demonstrate that the small peoples of the Caucasus did not only take from Byzantium, they also gave, and gave a good deal. Zwarthnotz is evidence.

A Monastery on the Shores of Lake Sevan

The classical age of Armenian architecture came to an end in the seventh century. In the eighth, under Arab rule, very little was built and even existing castles, palaces and churches suffered considerable damage. The end of the ninth century saw a revival under the Bagratid rule, closely linked with Armenia's newly-regained independence. As was to be expected, most of the new buildings were erected in Ani, the capital, but a considerable amount of building also went on at the same time in other regions. The monastery built on a peninsula jutting into the waters of Lake Sevan serves as an example.   82

The last great age of mediaeval architecture in Armenia lasted from the twelfth to the fourteenth century. Secular architecture made considerable progress, but the number of monasteries scattered in the picturesque highlands also increased considerably.

The monastery buildings, two churches and the ruins of a pronaos can be seen from afar, between the mountains, standing on the hilly peninsula extending into Lake Sevan.

Tradition has it that the monastery was built as early as the fourth century, though this is open to doubt. Nothing has survived from that period. The two similar churches still surviving, with medium-sized central domes and three apses each, were built during the Middle Ages, the smaller one, St. Karapet (St. John the Baptist), in the ninth century, the larger, Arakelots (the Holy Apostles), in A.D. 874. An inscription on the south   80–81
wall of Arakelots church and written sources relate that the monastery on the shores of the lake was founded anew by Mariam, Princess of Siuniki, in A.D. 874, but that building was still going on in the tenth and eleventh centuries. The waters of the lake have recently retreated; the monastery, in fact, which was built on an island, is now situated on a peninsula, and a road leads to it.

The church of Arakelots originally had a pronaos (zhamatun) on the western side, which is now a ruin. It possessed a timber roof and was adorned with carved columns, capitals and doors carved with popular subjects. The door of the Karapet church was also adorned with ornamented carvings. Some of these carved timber doors and capitals are preserved in the Historical Museum at Erivan.

The beautiful wooden door (Plate 137) was made in 1137, and originates from another ancient monastery, the famous Mush, on the shores of Lake Van. It was the door of the church dedicated to the Holy Apostles. It is easy to recognize the connection between the carved capitals and doors, and the characteristic Armenian folk motifs of these two churches.

Haghartsin Monastery

Haghartsin monastery, an eleventh century foundation, is set in fine mountain scenery, 18 km to the north of Dilizhan, a spa which boasts a splendid climate. The monastery, which is far from human habitation, is surrounded by ancient forests. The Haghartsin valley can be approached from the Tiflis main road, but to reach it involves a 6 km walk. The majestic forest, the beeches and oaks and shrubs, the smell of the flowers, and the splendid fresh mountain and forest air amply compensate for the length of the journey.

83-84 The monastery of Haghartsin was an average-size enclave. It consisted of three churches, two pronaos (one in ruins), a refectory, chapels, and a whole series of administrative buildings.

85 The Astvatsatsin Church, which was the principal church, stands to the north of the other buildings almost in isolation. There has been a great deal of discussion over the meaning

94 of the inscription above the southern gate, but the opinion of Professor N. M. Tokarski has finally been accepted. According to him this church, consecrated to the Holy Mother

95-99 of God, was built in 1281, and not in 1071, as some had maintained. The ground-plan is cruciform, the ornamentation is exceptionally beautiful and niches break the south

103 and north walls. Arcades run round the drum on which the dome rests, and this further heightens and emphasizes the fact that it is somewhat elongated.

104-106 Bas-reliefs, depicting two monks, the church and doves, decorate the east front. The pronaos used to be on the west side of the church. Its ruins are still visible, but the year of its construction is unknown.

Two further churches stand to the south of the Astvatsatsin Church, on the very edge of the precipice. The one consecrated to St. Gregory is the older, built in the eleventh century of roughly worked limestone. The octagonal drum of the dome is visible from afar. There are remains of wall-paintings on the inside. The architectural design of St. Gregory recalls buildings of earlier centuries, and in particular those of the tenth century. It is possible that this was the first church of what was originally a much more modest monastery. In the west there is a pronaos next to the church. The rectangular building was erected by the Princes Ivan and Zahar, members of the Zaharid family, towards the end of the twelfth or the beginning of the thirteenth century. The pronaos is slightly elongated, with a low arched drum supporting the dome, a tent-shaped roof with an opening to let in the light. The outer walls are plain and smooth and only the western entrance gate boasts a decorated protective projection over it. On the other hand, the interior is decorated with asymmetric patterns. The various architectural elements and reliefs (human figures, fantastic birds, rosettes etc.) differ from one another in a rich medley of designs.

St. Stephen's stands to the east of St. Gregory. This little basilica-type church was built *102* of blue basalt in 1244. It was probably a family chapel, a small-scale replica of the cathedral, used exclusively by the princely family. The charm, the delicate construction, the delicious miniature dome of this building and the bright natural colour of the stone tend to inspire a particular and almost personal affection for this small church.

Master Minas built the refectory of Haghartsin monastery in 1248. We know nothing *86–87* about him as a builder, but his work speaks for him. This refectory is one of the pearls of mediaeval architecture in Armenia. The refectory, with its simple exterior, stands a little apart, and was built by Master Minas at the time of the Mongol invasions. It was also very probably used for secular purposes as well. It was the hall where the Princes of Dolgoruki, whose domains included Haghartsin, received their visitors. The fever for building that dominated those centuries must be seen as a complex and peculiar competition existing between the religious and temporal powers. With trade and industry flourishing despite periodic invasion, and the church steadily extending its possessions, a sound economic base existed for widespread building and competition between the church and the feudal powers.

The form of the refectory is simple. It is of medium height, in its appearance more like a low building following the lines of the ground (21.6 metres long and 9.05 metres wide). The mastery of the builder is seen in the bold construction and majestic conception of the interior. He developed new architectural forms, spanning the interior space without the help of central columns. The refectory is covered by massive cross-vaulting. The heavy, imposing cross-vaulting rests on supporting piers and half-columns attached to the walls, and on corbels on the walls. These half-columns supporting the spring of the arch along the wall are very low, and as a result the vaulting truly takes wing, and appears to float in the air. The visitor cannot but be fascinated by this tangible realization of a single, monumental architectural conception. *88–89*

The interior is one large hall, with nothing to break its spatial unity, even though it is planned as two sections, since it is divided by two columns in the middle. The genius of the architect is displayed in the manner in which he has designed the sections as one, the parts being superbly integrated in the whole. There is no ornamentation in the interior of the refectory, the beauty of the cross-vaulting dominates the whole, each of the two sections possessing its own system of cross-vaulting, one of the sections being covered by stalactite vaulting. A low stone bench runs along the walls, brightening the impetuous spring of the arcading. Openings for light crown these two square interior spaces. National architectural traditions are renewed in this masterpiece; the shape is derived from the old ancient rectangular Armenian dwelling.

100–101 Many beautiful hachkars or stone crosses can be found in the monastery. Two of them, the tombstones of King Sembat and King Gagik, stand outside the south wall of the pronaos of St. Gregory. Ruins of chapels can be seen in the distance.

Parts of the monastery were restored by the Armenian Office for the Protection of Ancient Monuments in 1936.

The Monastery of Goshavank (Nor-Getik)

Goshavank or Nor-Getik monastery is 23 km from Dilizhan, a famous Armenian spa mentioned before.

The village of Kosh lies at an altitude of 1250 metres. Dense forests and bare rocky mountains surround it. The monastery stands on a hillside beside the village. Its foundation, as well as that of several other magnificent buildings, is connected with the name of Mechithar Kosh. Mechithar Kosh was one of the greatest thinkers, writers, poets, story-tellers, jurists, architects and scholars of mediaeval Armenia. He lived from 1133 to 1213. He can rightly be called one of the great figures of the Armenian proto-Renaissance. The *Book of Laws* which he edited bears witness to his progressive spirit. It proclaims that men were born free, and that only the limited availability of land and water led to their dependence on the mighty. This great man supported a centralized monarchy, denounced both the anarchy of the landed magnates and peasant rebellions, although he disapproved of the impoverishment of the peasantry. The academy founded by Mechithar Kosh, like others in the monasteries of Armenia, became an important centre in scholarship in the thirteenth century. Many scholars, including theologians and historians, studied within its walls. Kiriakos of Gandzak, the famous historian, was one of them.

The grandeur of the Armenian monasteries is not due to the size of the buildings, nor to their profusion, but to the nobility of the architecture itself, and the inspired choice of location. They fit into the surrounding mountainous landscape as if organically part of it. Set in high mountains among dense forests, the natural colours of bare rock emerging here and there, the sight of these centuries-old monastery walls provide the experience of a lifetime.

The twelfth and thirteenth century buildings at Goshavank served both ecclesiastical and secular purposes.

Mechithar Kosh built the Astvatsatsin Church, dedicated to the Holy Mother of God, between 1191 and 1196. It is cruciform with a central dome, the interior is divided by four clustered columns, with no side-altars in the western nave. The external walls are plain and unornamented, with the exception of the south and east fronts each broken by two triangular niches. The dome is massive, its small windows helping to give it the appearance of a keep. Its only ornament is a carved stone frieze running right round the drum of the dome. The building, façade and porch of the cathedral taken as a whole echo the ancient style of Armenian monasteries. The building is solid and low, and this

Bird ornamentation from an illuminated Gospel made in Jelegis, 1297
Matenadaran, Codex No. 7482

Ornamentation with lion and head of ox from a Gospel, 1287
Cilicia school
Matenadaran, Codex No. 197

Ornamentation from an illuminated Gospel, end of 13th c.
Cilicia school
Matenadaran, Codex No. 9422

Entry into Jerusalem
Detail of miniature from an illuminated Gospel, 1297
By Gregory of Tathev, 1378
Matenadaran, Codex No. 7482

is to its advantage, since the rocky plateau on which it is built is limited in extent and the church is backed by a precipice a few metres away, a steep hill rising on the other side. The zhamatun (the pronaos) inevitably found in these churches, is to the west of the building, and forms its only entrance. The light enters with difficulty through the openings in the roof and the magnificently proportioned interior is bathed in obscurity. The stone walls are covered with carvings and the multitude of crucifixes verge on confusion. There is an altar in the southern and north-eastern corners respectively of the pronaos. It is interesting that the extent of the pronaos is larger than the ground-plan of the church. This is understandable, since the pronaos served secular as well as ecclesiastical purposes. It served as the meeting place of the local population for certain occasions and events of great social importance.

St. Gregory's is to the south of the Astvatsatsin Church. It is not unlike the principal church, and was built in 1241, at the time of the Abbot Martyros. The church is in ruins, the dome has collapsed, but even in this condition, it is still an imposing sight.

St. Gregory the Illuminator's or the Little Church was built in 1237. It was erected by Prince Gregory Tha, a rich magnate, who was the confidant of Zahar Dolgoruki, the famous warlord, and acted as his executor. Prince Gregory Tha also completed the building of St. Gregory.

The church is not large and in composition reminds one of the early basilica with a single nave. It is vaulted, with an apse at the east end, and is precisely similar in form to the basilica-type churches so numerous in Armenia. But the splendid forms of the principal façade and porch give it an important place among the buildings at Goshavank. Indeed, in so far as ornamentation goes, it can compete with the churches of the 'Armenian Pompeii', Ani, the former capital.

Some argue that it owed its splendid decorations to Prince Gregory Tha's desire to outshine the capital. It is quite possible that this was so, although there are no documents extant to support this view. What is certain, however, is that the pursuit of picturesque effects was already a dominating trend when Prince Gregory Tha ordered the Church of St. Gregory the Illuminator to be built. This picturesque decoration is one of the achievements of thirteenth century building in Armenia. Ordinary visitors and scholars alike are fascinated by the shape of the façade, and by the delicate lacework of the stone. Scholars in particular admire the superb carving which recalls the complicated patterns and geometrical designs of eastern rugs.

The traditions of Armenian stone-carving came to maturity in the thirteenth century. The movement for picturesque effects in architecture succeeded in producing works more than equal to those of preceding ages, and though the scale of the churches is smaller, the effect on the onlooker is as great as that of tenth and eleventh century buildings. One cannot but disagree with those who claim to discover a decline of architecture in the growth of ornamentation and the lessened scale. It is probable that building on a large scale ceased as a consequence of the Seljukid and Mongol invasions, but the Armenian architects made sure that the churches would not lose their powers of attraction. The clover plant, together with geometrical motifs, is frequently used in the ornamentation. The design which frames the porch shows single stars, rows of stars, and a star in the intertwining foliate designs above the gate. The symbol of eternity shines in the arched vaulting of the gate. The two equally large, round, perfectly carved ornaments have given rise to a great deal of speculation. Some claim to recognize in them symbols of the sun, but others consider them purely geometrical designs.

This small undomed church is one of the most splendid developments of the legacy of the Ani school, and nothing can spoil its value, not even the over-elaborate and somewhat overcrowded and not quite successful impression given by the interior. The east wall, facing the hill, contains a double window of a most original design.

Two hachkars—stone crosses—stood beside the entrance to the small church. In fact, one is now in the Erivan Museum, and the other stands alone on the original site.

The beautifully carved stone cross is the work of Master Pavghos, whose remains rest 107–108 within the precincts of the monastery. Of all the many thousands of hachkars to be found on Armenian soil, this one, carved in 1291, may well be considered the most beautiful. It stands on a high plinth. It is a series of variations in grey, a pattern of stone lace washed by the rain, swept by the winds, scarred by the sun. The cross, the symbol of Christ's suffering, is in the centre. The cross as a whole can be likened to a flower springing from a seed, surrounded by intertwined vegetation. The symbol of the sun-disk is visible under the cross, but the lacy pattern divides it into twelve parts, and not the usual four or six. It is possible that this is a pagan symbol, though the sun-disk was also adopted as a symbol of the new god after the triumph of Christianity.

The hachkar is set in a frame of nine eight-pointed stars on both sides, each of them a small gem of differently patterned foliate ornamentation. Two designs—at the bottom of each side — are patterned on a cross. The hachkar is surmounted by a cornice and small projection with geometrical and foliate patterns.

Armenian stonemasons still work with the simplest of tools, hammers and chisels of various sizes, and are still masters in the art of dealing with soft tufa and hard granite. Nor should the library and campanile of the monastery of Goshavank be ignored, particularly as they are the precursors of the turret-shaped mausoleum-churches that made their appearance in Armenia early in the fourteenth century. The latest research shows that turret-shaped mausoleums had already appeared in Armenia as early as the tenth and eleventh centuries. A relatively small vaulted corridor connects the principal church and this building. Scholars are inclined to differ; some think the mausoleum was on the ground floor, and this seems more likely, others again consider that this was where the library was situated, and that the pronaos next door, which is now in ruins, was used as a reading-room. This is a problem which will prove difficult to solve but it is certain that in their heyday the mausoleum, the library, and the campanile above them must have made an imposing picture. Only part of the campanile can be seen today; the rotunda of the campanile has collapsed.

This complex structure was not built all at once. The ground floor was built before 1241, the campanile and the rotunda in 1291. The outside wall of the building is constructed of roughly worked stone, and the building is roofed by cross-vaulting. The façade is completely plain; it may well have been planned to decorate the plain walls with carvings, but the opportune moment never arrived. A staircase designed with some originality is built into the west front of the library and campanile.

A certain contradiction in the architectural design only emphasizes the festive appearance of the library and campanile at Goshavank. The heavy masses of the lower sections contrast with the lightly flowing proportions of the top of the campanile, reaching upward to the heights. In a relatively small area the gifted builders succeeded in producing a majestic and noble building by original and individual means.

The lonely chapel of Ripsime lies some way off from the complex of monastery buildings, towards the south-east, on the hillside below a dense forest.

The Monastery of Ayrivank (Geghard)

The road to the famous monastery of Ayrivank, lying roughly 40 km from the capital in a south-easterly direction, takes us through shady orchards, always upwards into the mountains, along the Erivan–Garni road. It passes through picturesque Armenian villages. Their names have a peculiar ring to them: Avan, Vochaberd, Gehadir and Garni. Leaving Garni behind, the road reaches the picturesque and beautiful steep valley of Geghard.

Written chronicles and popular tradition place the foundation of the monastery of Ayrivank in the first days of Christianity in Armenia, that is, in the fourth century. The Catholicos Ioann mentions Ayrivank, where he took refuge from the Arabs when he fled from the town of Dvin. But in their own good time the Arabs reached Ayrivank and destroyed it, and this, as told by the Catholicos-historian, happened in the ninth and tenth centuries.

The monastery was called Ayrivank, that is 'the monastery of caves', since caves cut into the rocks served as habitations there already in ancient times. Beginning with the thirteenth century, the name under which the monastery was mentioned was changed to Geghard, taken from the spear which pierced the side of Christ on the cross, and which was a holy relic preserved in this monastery.

The present buildings date from the twelfth and thirteenth centuries. Earlier buildings undoubtedly existed, but they have not survived.

The estates of the great aristocratic families grew in size and number as the Arab empire declined and the Seljukid Turks were, at least in part, expelled. The Princes Ivan and Zahar Dolgoruki were gifted generals serving Queen Tamar of Georgia, and the expulsion of the Seljuks and the foundation of the Zaharid dynasty in Armenia is linked to their name. The Orbelian and Prosian families were equally wealthy, and like the Zaharids, enriched Armenia with the buildings they erected. Ayrivank monastery is a typical building of the Zaharid period.

The Astvatsatsin Church, the principal church of the monastery, was built by Prince Ivan and Prince Zahar in 1215. Barsek Miaynakyac was the abbot at the time. The contemporary inscription on the church wall testifies to the fact, and also to the fact that a number of persons contributed towards the building of the church and that the side-altars were built by certain donors at their own expense. The Armenian inscription over the west door is a decoration in itself, and heightens the ornamentation of the façade. The principal church is an important example of the thirteenth century interior cruciform plan of Armenian church with a dome. There is a semicircular altar, constructed on mounting levels, at the east end, the south and east walls are adorned with high niches on the exterior, and the north wall is supported by the hillside.

The form and decoration of the walls is characteristic of the twelfth and thirteenth centuries. The façade, the porch and the drum of the dome are profusely decorated.

112 The Zaharid family arms surmount the main entrance: a lion attacking a bull. The lion symbolizes royal might, courage, strength of character and justice. It is an old favourite motif of Near Eastern origin, spread by the diffusion of Byzantine and other textiles and by illuminated manuscripts. The door jamb of the entrance is carved in a medley of peacocks, plant motifs, grapes and pomegranates delicately interlaced. As the sun moves the tufa changes colour and offers ever-changing impressions to the visitor.

113-114 The two peacocks facing each other above the door symbolize majesty and immortality. The grape and vine are the symbols of Christ, signifying in the age-old memories of the
115-116 people a prosperous harvest, wealth and happiness. Many consider the pomegranate to be a decorative element of Arab or Moorish origin; the truth is that it was they who transmitted it to Europe, but the motif itself is much older and occurs in the Caucasus as early as the seventh century.

117-118 The use of vertical lines dominates the architectural composition of the church. This impression is increased by the height of the drum of the dome, and by the vertical arrangement of the ornamentation on the façade. The wall is broken into narrow compartments which increase the sense of the vertical. The high dome and its elongated drum are richly decorated, surrounded by a blind arcade resting on half-columns, together with reliefs of birds and animals, lacework patterns in stone and a peculiar chain motif. The more one studies them, the more something is revealed, such as the beautifully worked head of a small girl hardly perceived under the cross on the dome. The birds and animals on the drum invite all sorts of speculation. The head of an ox is a popular motif dating back to pagan times, as well known in the Caucasus as elsewhere. It is the symbol of the sacrificial animal, but also of St. Luke. The lamb on the other hand symbolizes patience and docility, or perhaps is merely inspired by the fact that the raising of fat lambs is one of the sources of plenty in this area.

Grey-yellow, variants of brown, elsewhere a blackish or yellowish shade all combine in the subtle colouring of the outer walls, more darkly shaded where exposed to the wind and weather. When the sun shines the colours of the church walls glow; in dull weather they radiate a sombre majesty. The pictorial effect is increased by the ornamentation of the façade, since the Armenian stonemasons were skilled in exploiting the play of light and shade on all the different modulations of colour in the stone.

The interior of the church has been blackened by candle fumes and incense smoke, by the moisture in the air and by the hand of time itself. The atmosphere is heightened and festive. The visitor is encompassed by the darkness of the smoke and air of centuries. The sun finds it difficult to penetrate through the narrow windows in the drum of the dome, and the walls are hidden in semi-darkness. Mediaeval architects were experts in lighting techniques, and narrow, small windows placed in every second arcade provide for an even distribution of light.

Two hachkars (stone crosses) stand on plinths to the right of the entrance to the principal church. The crosses face west, and the faithful face east during worship; that, surely, was the underlying principle in positioning the hachkars. There are several rows of hachkars on the rock face behind the church, eloquent in their beauty. Some have been set into the rock face, others carved straight out of it.

A small decorative fountain stands to the right of the church, in the courtyard of the monastery. Its water is as cold as ice and crystal clear. Fountains are very popular with the Armenians. The taste for fountains goes back thousands of years. Water is literally the fountain of life. Nothing can be produced in this type of country without irrigation. The ground is stony and infertile, the heat of the sun is unbearable, every drop of water is precious, and the fountains therefore have a symbolic significance. They were built to honour fallen heroes, and there is no superfluous ornamentation or elaboration, the architecture and the flowing, refreshing water are expressive and memorial enough.

The zhamatun (pronaos) at Ayrivank is one of the most beautiful and most interesting *127–128* buildings in Armenia. Its prototype was the ancient four-columned Armenian peasant house, with an opening in the centre of the roof. The pronaos first appeared in Armenian architecture in the tenth and eleventh centuries and came to full maturity between the twelfth and thirteenth centuries. It has a secular appearance, and indeed its purpose was only in part ecclesiastical. The pronaos at Ayrivank, as was usual, was attached to the west wall of the church. It was a meeting place for church and lay councils. Those who found no place inside the church stood there during the service, and the pronaos also housed the tombs of a number of outstanding personalities. That is where the members of the aristocratic families that built the monastery were buried.

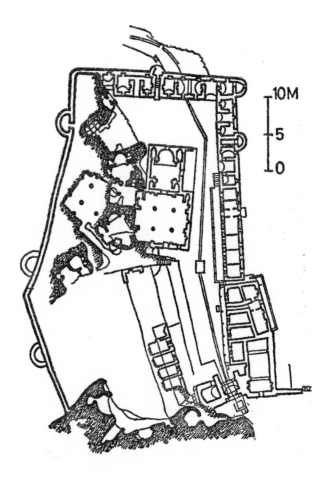

*Geghard. Ground-plan
of the Ayrivank monastery*

The famous zhamatun at Ayrivank was built between 1225 and 1230. The natural rock of the mountain forms its north wall. Four massive columns divide the rectangular space into nine sections. The first and central part is the largest, the other eight are smaller. Arcades link the space between the columns and support the roof. The vaulting is not the same throughout. Cross-vaulting is used, as well as other types of vaulting.

131–133 The central section is the most beautiful and most important. It forms the axis of the building. On stepping into the zhamatun one's eye is drawn to the ceiling and the beauty of its stalactite vaulting. Armenian master builders produced many different types of roofs, but one of the most beautiful forms is undoubtedly the stalactite vaulting of the central space, which the Armenians took over from the Moslem peoples of the East, and used with genius. The light of the sun, pouring in through the central opening in the vaulting, increases the artistic effect. Professor N. M. Tokarski, the famous Leningrad historian of architecture, has aptly described this masterpiece of mediaeval Armenian art as 'sculpture of architecture'. The walls and columns are covered in religious inscriptions, exhorting and prescribing, and the usual hachkars, or stone crosses, are present.

134–135 Some stand beside the wall, others are carved into the walls of the pronaos.

The architect made use of all the achievements of his predecessors to make of the building a symbol of the experience of centuries. The only ornamentation on the simple, geometrically designed outside of the building is in the vaulting of the porch and a campanile standing at one of the corners; the inside, on the other hand, is as lovely as a fairy tale.

S. H. Mnatsakanian, the Armenian historian of architecture, has demonstrated that previously prepared stone slabs were used in the construction of this complex building. The mediaeval master-masons worked with seven different types of hewn stone.

The most interesting period in the architectural history of Ayrivank is the time when Prince Prosh of the Khaghbakjan clan bought the monastery from the Zaharids in the thirteenth century, and proceeded to build the famous cave churches.

Two passages through the north wall of the zhamatun, which, as we already mentioned, is formed by the rock face itself, lead to the cave churches carved out of the rock.

The entrance on the left, western side leads into the first church carved into the rock. It is called Avazan, and Galdzak the master builder was commissioned to build it in 1283 by Prince Prosh, as an inscription on the wall relates.

The ground-plan is that of a mutilated cross, the ceiling is the stalactite cross-vaulting typical of the thirteenth century, with a central opening for light. There are some fine stone-carvings in the dome, and the name of the brilliant architect, Galdzak, is cut into the ornamentation of the ceiling under the central opening.

The cave church was built, or rather carved out of the rock where a 'holy spring' had *123–126* already existed in ancient times (its name: Avizan, means baptismal font). The clear water still bubbles up in one of the corners of the church, and tradition has it that those who throw money into it will have their wish gratified and return to Ayrivank one day.

This church in the rocks, though nothing more than a cave made by human hands, is a *129–130* perfect replica of a stone building. It is a facsimile of the architectural form of buildings of a similar type. There is cross-vaulting and a stalactite-vaulted dome. The large niches echo the niches found in contemporary secular buildings. Galdzak and his stonemasons had to exercize the greatest care. Every movement of the chisel was important. Spoiled work could not be replaced, as with an ordinary building. The architect was familiar with every nuance in the working of tufa. He handled this familiar building material to perfection and left a masterpiece to posterity. Historians of architecture believe that a shaft was first sunk and the churches were then carved to represent rays.

Entry into Jerusalem
Detail of miniature from an illuminated Gospel, 1297
Vaspurakhan school
Matenadaran, Codex No. 4867

Christic on the Cross
Detail of miniature by Gregory of Tathev from an illuminated Gospel, 1297
Matenadaran, Codex No. 7482

The second cave church also boasts a pronaos (zhamatun), through which it can be reached. The small pronaos has a rectangular ground-plan, and probably served as the family tomb of Prince Prosh. The arms of the Khaghbakjan clan, Prince Prosh's family, is visible above the arcade, and is a noble and masterly piece of carving. Even in the semi-darkness one can see that the relief depicts a bull's head, holding ropes in its mouth with lions tied to their ends. An eagle with half-opened wings can be seen between the two lions. The eagle carries a lamb in its claws. The lion symbolizes power, might and justice, the eagle eternity and resurrection. They were the favourite heraldic beasts of the Middle Ages. They reach back to ancient and pagan times and are akin to folk art and certain totem symbols used by the ancient Armenian tribes.

121–122

On sunny days it is possible to see the stonework in the chapel, which is invisible when the weather is cloudy and the light is not good. The sign of eternity, two combined wheels, is cut on the east wall, together with a number of pictures of sirens. These faces barely sketched into the rock wall are intensely human; one, with bitter features, is weeping, another is smiling. The play of light and shade reveals the power of these old Armenian masons to bring the dead stone to life.

The second cave church, dedicated to the Holy Mother of God, follows the pronaos. This cave has been constructed in the form of a basilica with a dome. Semicircular arcades support the dome. Twelve blind windows have been placed between paired half-columns. Lacework designs in stone under the opening for light complete the arrangement. There are stone crosses on both sides of the altar.

119–120

Steep steps cut in the rock face lead up to the second level of cave buildings in the monastery courtyard. They were constructed by Prince Papak, Prosh's son, and Ruzukan, his wife. According to the inscription on the north-eastern column work began in 1288, and took two years. The burial vault is reached at the end of a fairly long corridor. The walls are covered with crosses carved into the rock. The corridor ends in a rectangular room recalling a zhamatun, where four massive columns and arcades support the ceiling. The dome in the ceiling of the burial vault has an opening letting in the light. The walls here are also covered with hachkars or stone crosses, and inscriptions in the Armenian script that form part of the decoration in themselves.

The acoustics in the cave churches and the burial vaults are superb. This is in fact true of all the Armenian churches. The sound was improved by large pottery vessels which the mediaeval architects built into the dome.

Matenadaran

Masterpieces of illumination were preserved at Echmiadzin, the ancient home of the intellectual and cultural life of Armenia. The Matenadaran, set up in the fifth century, came under the direct supervision of the Patriarch of the Armenian Church, and, during the whole of its existence, lasting nearly 1,500 years, faithfully served the cause of Armenian education. The word 'matenadaran' means 'library' in Old Armenian, and the archives of Armenian manuscripts and codices at Erivan have retained the old name; in 1920 the archives at Echmiadzin were nationalized and reorganized as the Echmiadzin State Scientific Research Archives Institute, and later, in 1939, moved to the capital, Erivan.

The Matenadaran, which bears the name of Mesrop Maschots, serves as the archives where whatever survives of Armenian literature is preserved, and, at the same time, as a research institute. The manuscripts preserved there provide valuable material not only for research into the emergence and development of Armenian culture, but also into a fuller knowledge of the history and culture of the peoples of the Caucasus and the Near East. Scriptoria were attached to all the greater monasteries and religious academies; the works of Armenian writers and scholars were duly transcribed, the works of foreign authors translated. The devoted labours of these scribes have preserved many a rare ancient exemplars of Armenian history, philosophy, literature and medicine for our study. The works of a number of ancient and mediaeval authors, moreover, can be found only in Armenian translation, the originals being long lost.

Wars, plunder and vandalism destroyed precious Armenian manuscripts by the thousands. At a rough estimate some 25,000 Armenian manuscripts are to be found in foreign museums and libraries throughout the world; the finest are in Vienna, Paris, London, Venice and Jerusalem. In the Matenadaran of Erivan more than 10,000 manuscripts and nearly 4,000 manuscript fragments are catalogued, in addition to more than 100,000 old documents.

In the Foreign Languages Department of the Matenadaran are preserved Arabic, Persian, Greek, Latin, Georgian, Old Slavonic, Polish and many other foreign manuscripts. The Department of Incunabula contains the first Armenian book printed in Armenian, a 'Calendar', which was printed in Venice in 1512 by Hakop, the first Armenian printer.

The oldest codex, the Lazarev Gospel, dates from A.D. 887. Only fragments from the fifth to eighth centuries A.D. have come down to us. These ancient manuscripts were written on parchment; the earliest manuscript written on paper dates from A.D. 981, and contains a number of miscellaneous writings on philosophy and astronomy.

The most interesting and rare Armenian manuscripts can be seen in the well-arranged permanent exhibitions of the Matenadaran, and the codices of various sizes and forms well repay study. The largest codex is the Mush book of festive sermons, transcribed by a monk between A.D. 1201 and 1204. It weighs 32 kilograms, and is 51 by 70 cm in size. The smallest is a 'Calendar' dating from 1436. It weighs only 19 gramms, and is only 3 by 4 cm in size.

Works on almost all the subjects cultivated in antiquity and the Middle Ages are to be found in the Matenadaran. Most are on historical subjects; works by some eighty historians and chroniclers of ancient times cover the course of history from the fifth to the eighteenth century. The most famous fifth century work, *The Life of Mesrop Maschots*, written by the priest Koriun, is a biography of the creator of the Armenian alphabet. In his chronicle, *The History of Armenia*, Agathangelus gives an account of the spread of Christianity in Armenia and the neighbouring countries. In the work *The History of Vardan and the War of the Armenians*, the monk Elisaeus recorded the history of the popular uprising against the Persian conquerors and the battle of Avarair (May 26, A.D. 451). Moses of Chorene, the father of Armenian historiography, was the first to write a history of the Armenians and their ancestors from the antiquity to A.D. 428.

Works by more than thirty ancient and mediaeval philosophers are catalogued in the Matenadaran, although these represent only a moiety of those destroyed in the numerous wars fought over Armenia. The earliest date back to the fifth century. Elements of materialism are noticeably present in the works of the fifth century Jeznik Koghbetsi and the sixth century David Anaght. The great age of Armenian philosophical thinking was that of the eleventh to the fourteenth centuries. During this period the erudite professors of the famous religious seminary of Tathev are recognized as the greatest philosophers and mathematicians of mediaeval Armenia, the two most outstanding being Ioan Voronetsi and Gregory of Tathev.

The philosopher Hovhannes Sarkavag, who lived in the late eleventh and early twelfth centuries, attacked the question of the cognition of reality in his work *Polygonal Numbers*. The mediaeval jurists of Armenia, who from early times had begun to frame statutes and laws which took national, ecclesiastical, manufacturing and commercial interests into due consideration, also deserve a word. The Patriarch Hovhannes Odznetzi (A.D.

728) drew up the first Armenian code of laws, and in the twelfth century Mechithar Kosh, jurist and philosopher, drew up the first compilation of laws, which also contained regulations governing the practice and administration of the law.

Among the Armenian manuscripts are several on mathematics, astrology, chemistry, geography, cosmography and medicine. The seventh century Ananias of Shirak, a learned mathematician, astronomer and philosopher, despite the official disapproval of the clergy, explained the eclipse of the sun and the moon as well as the properties of the earth as a celestial body. It was also Ananias of Shirak who wrote one of the oldest scientific works on arithmetic. There are a great number of manuscripts on medicine also in the library, for there were hospitals and leper colonies in Armenia as early as the middle of the fourth century A.D. Mechithar Heratzi, Grigoris and Amirdovlat were famous mediaeval physicians. They wrote books on the anatomy of the human body, methods of treatment, the use of drugs, and the nature and course of different diseases. Old herbals are also preserved at Echmiadzin, in which the mediaeval apothecary described the properties of various herbs, accompanied by brightly coloured illustrations of the herb, tree or flower in question. The library also possesses old formularies in which alchemists, goldsmiths and other craftsmen wrote down the secrets of their trade. They include, for instance, a recipe for durable ink.

Mediaeval Armenia left a rich legacy of literature and poetry to posterity as well, for poems by more than two hundred poets have come down to us. Gregory of Narek, Nerses Shnorhali, Konstantin Jernkatzi, Hovhannes Tulkurantzi, Nagas Ovnatan and the great Sajat-Nova, writing from the tenth to the eighteenth century, sang in turn of mankind, truth, honesty, friendship and love.

The poets attacked the social abuses of the age, the evil, ignorance and greed of individuals, and the rapacity and despotism of the nobles. The poet Frik, who lived in the thirteenth century, spoke out courageously against social oppression in his works entitled 'Complaints' and 'The Wheel of Fortune'.

Music also flourished. There is a good deal of evidence that Armenian music had reached a high level of development even before the adoption of Christianity. The oldest hymns date from the third century A.D. Armenian religious music developed from the fourth century on, and drew on Syrian and Byzantine sources as well as the native traditions of the country. The Matenadaran possesses hundreds of specimens of mediaeval religious and secular songs, transcribed in a special musical notation.

The illuminated manuscripts of Armenia in the Matenadaran, with their rich variety of colour, original iconography and virtuosity of ornamentation, are particularly splendid.

The emergence and development of the art of illumination is a complicated process, and only knowledge of Armenian history and art can help us to understand this particular Armenian art, dating back more than a thousand years. For one thing the geographical situation of Armenia favoured the development of the Armenian arts. During the whole of its historical existence, the Armenian people were in direct contact with the Iranian, Hellenic, Byzantine and Arabic cultures, as well as the art of the Asian and Caucasian peoples. Commercial and cultural relations stimulated and developed the knowledge and craftsmanship of Armenian scholars, artists, and craftsmen.

As early as the sixth century the art of manuscript illumination flourished in Syria, and this may have helped to inspire the illumination and ornamentation of manuscripts in Armenia. The growth of a national Armenian life and the important role of the Church required the rapid spread of writing, the education of scribes and translators, and the translation of all types of religious and foreign works. Apart from the leaven of foreign influences there was also the stimulus provided by the native arts of Armenia itself, such as the seventh century mural paintings of the Lmbat and Aruts churches, the fifth century ornamental capitals of the Kasakh cathedral, the mosaics and reliefs of the Hellenistic age, and the remains of ancient Urartu painting.

Next to architecture, illuminated manuscripts and their miniatures probably represent the greatest Armenian contribution to art. Famous schools of illumination and scriptoria continued to turn out manuscripts century after century, and the masterpieces emanating from the scriptoria of Cilicia or the Hizan monastery probably exercized an influence on illumination in East and West alike.

It is indisputable that a close connection existed in Armenia between architecture, architectural ornamentation, and the decorative illumination of manuscripts. The same kind of connections may well have existed between fresco painting, panel painting and the art of illumination.

The large-scale archaeological excavations of recent decades have uncovered much in the way of remains of early Armenian art. Murals, fine carving in stone, stone crosses carved like lace, for instance, pottery and examples of goldsmith's work, and above all, architecture justify us in the belief that the art of manuscript illumination existed as early as the fifth and sixth centuries, although the earliest illuminated manuscript extant—the Lazarev Gospel—dates from the ninth century.

The Armenian illuminated manuscript possesses great artistic value in its own right, as well as providing a valuable source of raw material for the study of mediaeval Armenian history, architecture, ethnography, theatre, manufacturing, and even Armenian flora and fauna. The Armenian illuminators took their subject-matter and decorative motifs from the daily life around them, the remains of the ancient theatre, for example. The Greek historian, Plutarch, mentions in one of his works that in 69 B.C. the Armenian king Tigranes II had a theatre built in his new capital, Tigranokert. Other ancient historians also recorded that well before Christ Greek plays were performed in Armenian towns, and indeed theatrical performances continued to be put on in Armenia well into the Middle Ages, so it is not surprising that the miniatures in many numbers of manuscripts represent characteristic scenes from the theatre, actors in stage masks and costumes, with flowers or musical instruments in their hands.

Within the art of the manuscript as a whole various trends spontaneously developed; side by side with miniatures with an aristocratic appeal, designed for men of rank, appeared a popular school of illumination, using cruder colours and presenting the more realistic, familiar life of the common people.

Armenian ornamentation in general was organically connected with the art of illumination, as evidenced by the extraordinarily high standard of ornamentation in Armenian manuscripts with its great variety of animal, and abstract plant motifs.

It is hard to put into words the inexhaustible splendour of ornamentation that the imagination of the mediaeval Armenian masters conjured up on the page. All the animal grace of creatures from popular fables was employed to compose ornamental initials and letters; fish, cranes, storks and foxes, colourful running bands above the text, flowers and birds, decorated borders are found in page after page. The fairylands of East and West are reflected in them, set down with a practised ease, enormous skill and craftsmanship, and great artistry.

The miniatures of the famous Gospel of Echmiadzin, known throughout the world, were painted by the master illuminator Ioann in the famous Noravank monastery and probably modelled on illustrations in older Armenian gospels. He learned his art in the illuminators' school at Sjnik, but it also has connections with the scriptoria of the Tathev monastery as well; the colours of his miniatures are fresh and pure, his style grave and imposing. The ivory cover of this gospel, carved in relief, is a work of art in its own genre.

The names of a few mediaeval Armenian illuminators have been preserved in various sources. One of them is Master Gregory, the artist who painted the miniatures in the famous Gospel from Targmantsatz monastery in the first half of the thirteenth century, in the years preceding the Mongol invasion. Master Grigor may well have been one of the most important illuminators of his age, for all the developments of the preceding age fused in his works; his miniatures not only illustrated the text, but formed independent pictures according to his fancy. His range of colouring was rich and subtle, with a particular predilection for sombre blues, reds and browns. The faces of his figures are marked by subtle signs of suffering, the deep-set eyes speak with moving eloquence.

The illuminator Markare worked in the first decades of the thirteenth century. The miniatures of the Haghpat Gospel (1211) are ascribed to him. They are natural and direct, popular in their appeal, yet executed with great skill and care.

Toros Taronatzi was one of the greatest exponents of the Gladzor school of painting. The influence of the Cilicia school of painting can be seen in his work, but the strange beings, the scenes and colourful ornamentation which appear on the pages of the Gospel are original and independent in conception. There is St. George defeating the dragon, there is the eagle watching the partridge, there are demons hunted by angels, there are sirens, parrots, crocodiles. Parallel to the representation of the Virgin nursing her Child is the movingly symbolic painting of a hind giving suck to her fawn.

Master Momik lived in the first decades of the fourteenth century and also worked in the Gladzor monastery. An academy and scriptoria were attached to the monastery, and master Momik was not only a famous illuminator, but also a stone-carver. It was he who carved the fine stone cross in Noravank, and there is a particularly plastic, sculptural quality in his painting of miniatures.

The monastery of Tathev was one of the centres of Armenian knowledge and culture in the thirteenth and fourteenth centuries, and in fact continued to occupy this position in later centuries as well. Here lived and worked Gregory of Tathev, the famous philosopher and great illuminator. He did not illustrate many manuscripts, but one of them, written as early as 1297, was illuminated by him much later, in the last years of the fourteenth century. His choice of colouring was very original, based on the intermingling effects of mellow browns and blues, with a daring use of light yellows and lively reds.

In this manner his miniatures vividly recall the paintings in the Targmantsatz monastery's Gospel. There is a certain austere dignity, combined with delicacy of line, in his work.

Master Toros Roslin was, on the other hand, the greatest artist of the aristocratic Cilicia school of Armenian miniature painting. His work, of an extraordinary high quality, dates from the second half of the thirteenth century. We know nothing of his life; it is only graphically expressed in his work. His paintings, realistic in their approach, are dominated by a feeling for the things of this world, a predilection for the earthly life of mankind, and they are consequently permeated with a humanistic atmosphere. Toros Roslin's illuminated manuscripts are to be found in Jerusalem, Baltimore, Erivan and other cities, but only seven of the manuscripts signed with his name are authenticated; those attributed to him are much greater.

In Toros Roslin's work what is most striking is the display of colours, carefully and harmoniously composed against the basic gold tone of the pages of his miniatures, although he did not use it as much as many other illuminators. The aristocratic atmosphere of his works is defined by the use of gold leaf, the luxuriant ornamentation and the choice of strange and fantastic beings. He was excellent in the picturesque, almost plastic representation of plants and animals, and a master in the representation of the human form. His Virgin is feminine and slender, with a touch of the coquette; she wears elegant clothes, like the aristocratic women in Cilicia whom the artist knew well, and her attitude displays the self-confidence of the aristocrat. The grey blues and violets of her robe melt effectively together, the whole figure stands out against the glittering golden background. The pleats of the robe in particular reveal the hand of a master; the hems are decorated with gold, to enhance their formal effect.

Master Sarkis Pitzak was another artist from the Cilicia school of miniature painting, but in his time, in the fourteenth century, it was already showing signs of decline. Fifteen signed works of his are known. Among them is the Gospel illuminated by eight different illuminators, including the famous Toros Roslin, the whole under the control of Sarkis Pitzak. Pitzak painted a great number of miniatures himself, but his style is stiffer, and compared with Toros Roslin less universal, less open to nature and the world of people around him.

There are many legends on the life and work of these artists. *Pitzak* means wasp, and he is said to have earned this nickname because his visitors believed that a wasp in one of his drawings was alive.

St. Luke the Evangelist with Theophilus
Detail of miniature from an illuminated Gospel, 1287
Cilicia school
Matenadaran, Codex No. 197

Herdsman and animals
Detail of miniature from an illuminated Gospel, 1304
Nakhichevan school
Work of Master Simeon
Matenadaran, Codex No. 3722

With Hakob Djughajetzi, who lived and worked at the end of the sixteenth and the beginning of the seventeenth century, the Armenian art of illumination in fact came to an end. This gifted artist was forced to live abroad. He worked in New-Julfa, Persia, and made illustrations to the work *The History of Alexander the Great of Macedonia*, as well as to a Gospel transcribed in 1610. Although living abroad, he continued to be an Armenian, following the traditions and practice of the ancient Armenian art of illumination. His designs are delicate and elegant, his use of colour oriental, his ornamentation—although entirely Armenian in character—shows the strong influence of Persian motifs.

Throughout their stormy history the Armenian people cherished and protected the old illuminated manuscripts embodying their several thousand-year-old history and culture, knowing that only their ancient national culture defended them from mental subjugation and the spiritual domination of their enemies. The legacy of the Matenadaran was a source of their strength and a pledge of their rebirth, which is why the Matenadaran is the sacred hall of Armenian national culture today.

Bibliography

Bachmann, W.: *Kirchen und Moscheen in Armenien und Kurdistan*. Leipzig, 1913.

Strzygowski, J.: *Die Baukunst der Armenier und Europa*. Wien, 1918.

Macler, F.: *Documents d'art arménien*. I–II. Paris, 1924.

Baltrusaitis, J.: *Études sur l'art médiéval en Georgie et en Arménie*. Paris, 1929.

Свирин, А. Н.: *Миниатюра древней Армении*. Москва–Ленинград, 1939.

Пиотровский, Б. Б.: *История и культура Урарту*. Ереван, 1944.

Якобсон, А. Л.: *Очерки истории зодчества Армении V–XVII вв.* Москва–Ленинград, 1950.

Аракелян, Б. Н.: *Гарни*. I–III. Ереван, 1951, 1957, 1962.

Арутюнян, В. М.–Сафарян, С. А.: *Памятники армянского зодчества*. Москва, 1951.

Оганесян, К. Л.: *Зодчий Трдат*. Ереван, 1951.

Дурново, Л. А.: *Древнеармянская миниатюра*. Ереван, 1952.

Гоян, Г.: *Театр древней Армении*. I–II. Москва, 1952.

Тревер, К. В.: *Очерки по истории культуры древней Армении*. Москва–Ленинград, 1953.

Арутюнян, В.: *Звартноц*. Ереван, 1954.

Халпахчян, О. Х.: *Архитектура Армении. Всеобщая история архитектуры*. Т. III. Москва, 1958.

Schütz, Ö.: 'Armenien Hasar'. *Acta Orient. Hung.* VIII (Budapest), 1958.

Сахинян, А.: *Гарни и Гехард*. Москва, 1958.

Пиотровский, Б. Б.: *Ванское царство (Урарту)*. Москва, 1959.

Schütz, Ö.: 'Nicholas Misztótfalusi Kiss and Armenian book printing'. *Acta Orient. Hung.* IX (Budapest), 1959.

Akurgal, E.: *Die Kunst Anatoliens von Homer bis Alexander*. Berlin, 1961.

Hegyi, I.: *Elvarázsolt madarak. Örmény népmesék*. [Enchanted birds. Armenian folktales]. Budapest, 1961.

Токарский, Н. М.: *Архитектура Армении VI–XIV вв.* Ереван, 1961.

Abgarian, G. W.: *The Matenadaran*. Erivan, 1962.

Измайлова, Т.–Айвазян, М.: *Искусство Армении*. Москва, 1961.

Парсамян, В. А.: *История армянского народа*. Ереван, 1962.

Симонян, А. П.: *Ереван. Очерк истории, экономики и культуры города*. Ереван, 1965.

Dournovo, L. A.: *Miniatures arméniennes*. Erivan, 1967.

Арутюнян, В. М.: *Архитектурные памятники Эчмиадзина*. Ереван, 1968.

Historical Museum of Armenia—Guide-Book. M. Khondkarian–S. Amirian–J. Hovhannisian. Erivan, 1968.

Казарян, М.: *Художники Овнатаняни*. Москва, 1968.

Оганесян, К.: *Эребуни*. Ереван, 1968.

List of Plates

ECHMIADZIN

PARBI

ASHTARAK

ZWARTHNOTZ

SEVAN

HAGHARTSIN

GOSHAVANK

GEGHARD

The black-and-white photos
were made on Agfa (Leverkusen),
the coloured ones on
Agfa CT Professional rough material
with Zenza Bronica cameras
and Nikkor objectives.

Erebuni—Erivan

Karmir-Blur

16, 17, 18

27, 28, 29, 30,

Echmiadzin (Vagarshapat)

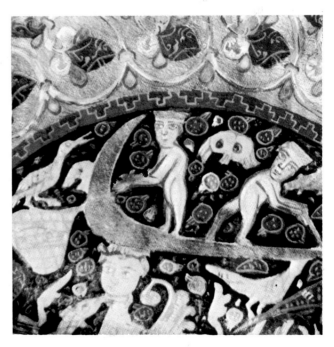

Parbi

63

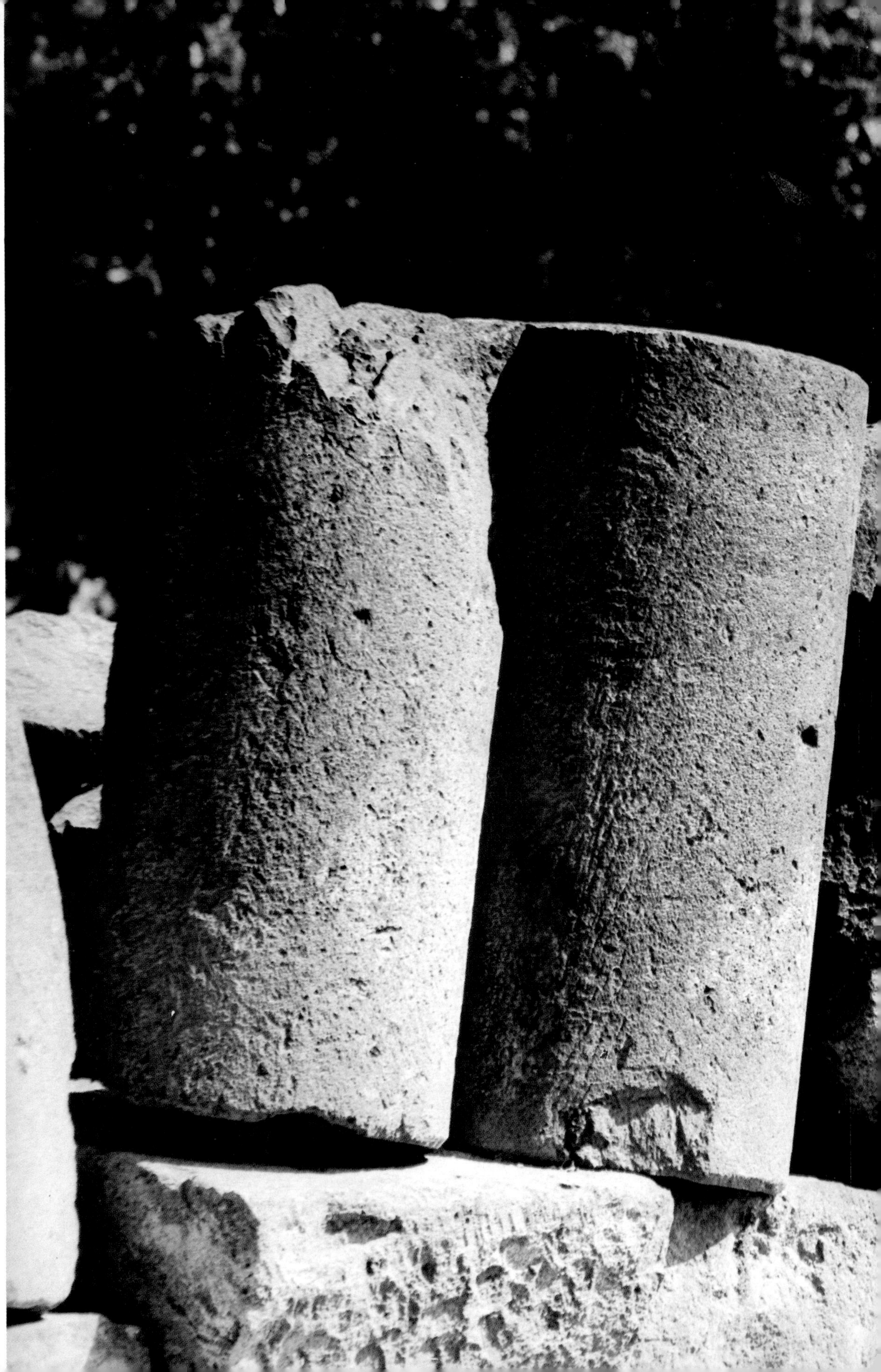

70, 71

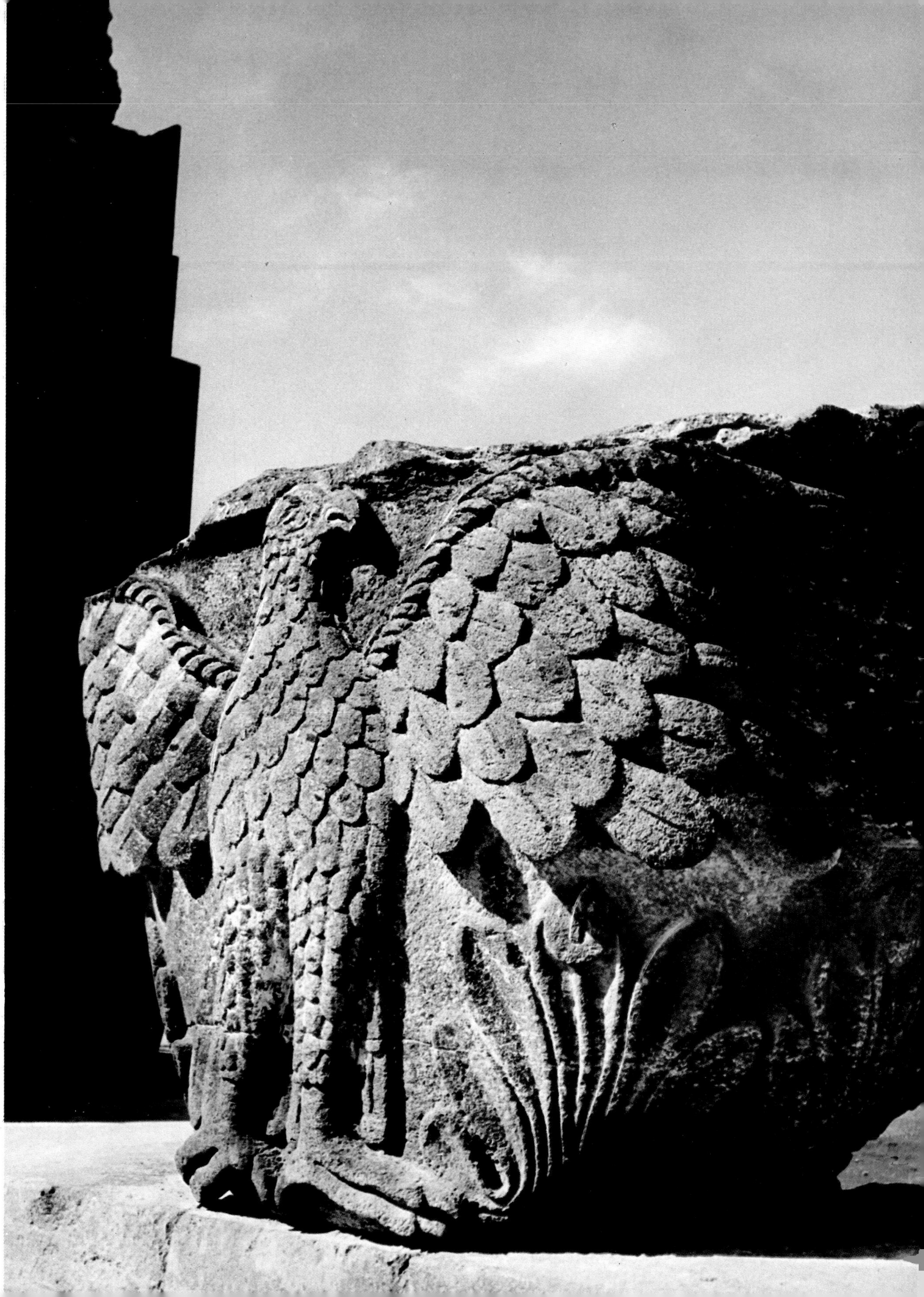

Sevan

104, 105, 106

Goshavank

Geghard (Ayrivank)

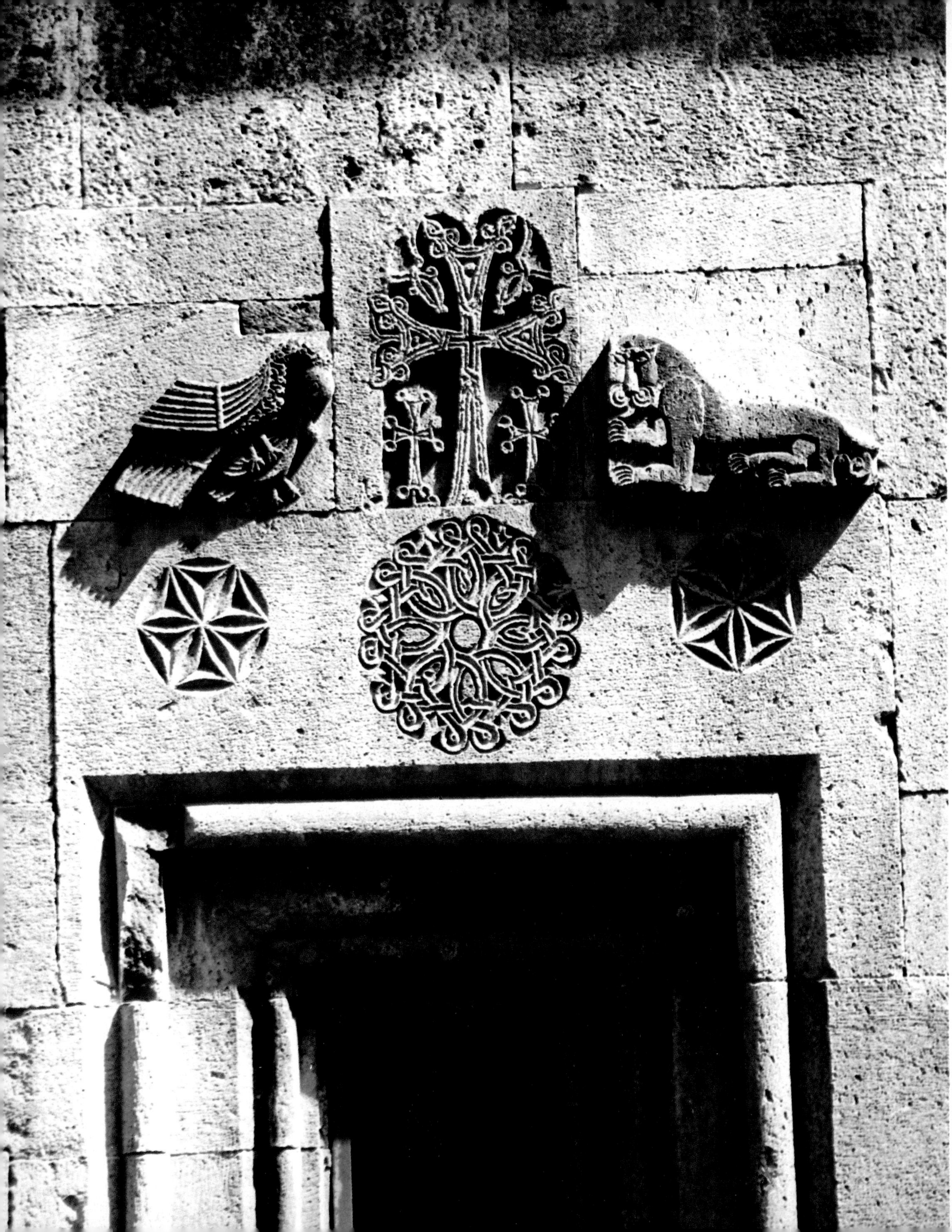

115
116

134
135

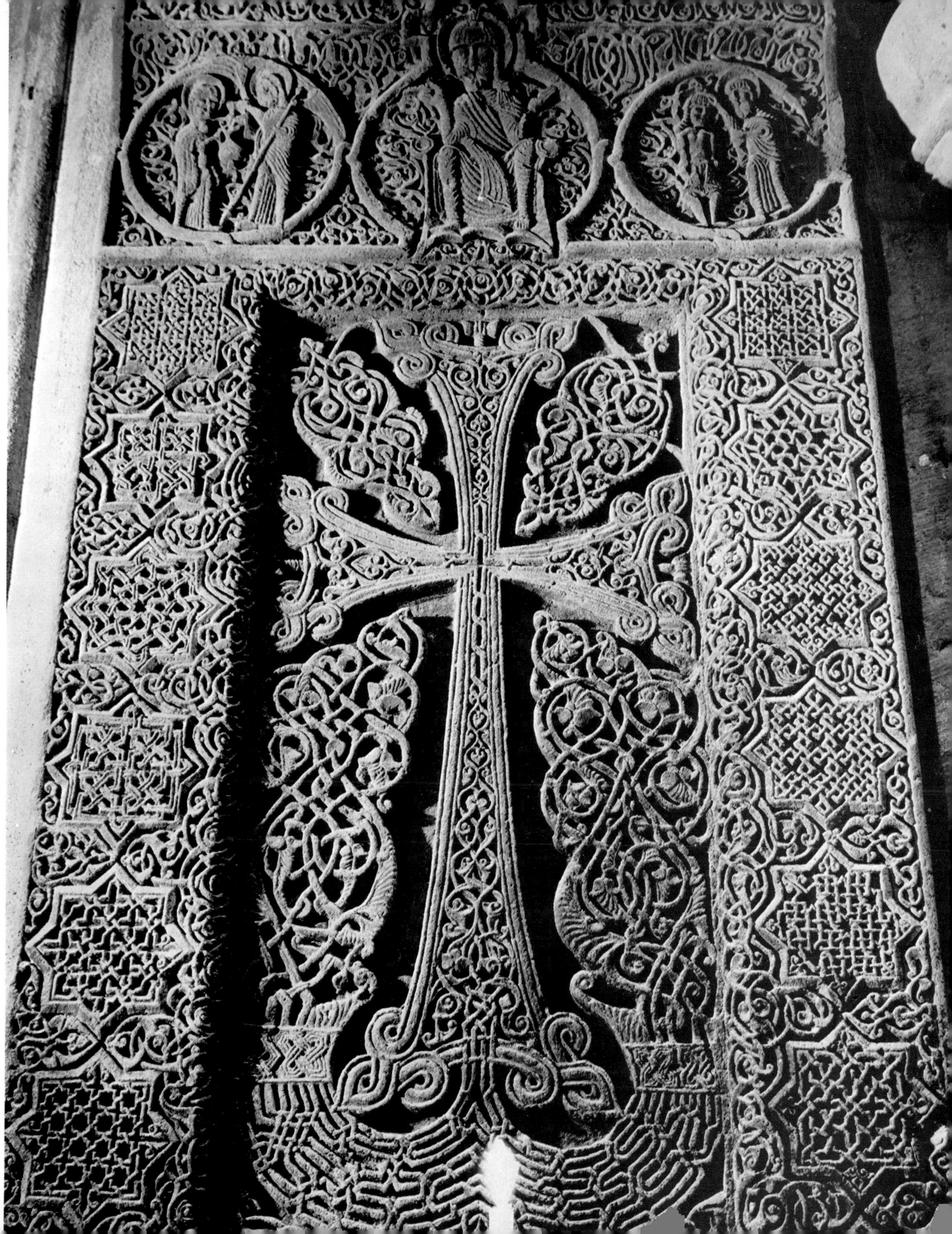